SOME PEOPLE WATCH CLOCKS TO TELL WHAT TIME IT IS, I WATCH PEOPLE TO KNOW WHAT TIME IT IS

CARL O. SNOWDEN

Order this book online at www.trafford.com
or email orders@trafford.com

Most Trafford titles are also available at major online book retailers.

Print information available on the last page.

ISBN: 978-1-4907-9927-8 (sc)
ISBN: 978-1-4907-9926-1 (e)

Trafford rev. 05/28/2020

 **www.trafford.com**
North America & international
toll-free: 1 888 232 4444 (USA & Canada)
fax: 812 355 4082

CONTENTS

PROLOGUE

Oprah G. Winfrey and
Carl O. Snowden

I remember when I was growing up, I believed anything was possible. In my child's world, my life was full of dreams. I believed nothing was impossible. When I became older, I began reflecting on my life. The following are some observations and those reflections.

Over the years, my journey has allowed me to meet many people who have in some way impacted my life with rewarding lessons and experiences. Some were famous and others were lesser known, but all added value to my view on life.

I've been driven by activism since I was a teenager and it has since been a core part of what has directed my path throughout my adult life. My activism led to various careers working for the media, local government and education.

During my years as an activist, I worked at WANN radio station in Annapolis, Maryland, WJZ-TV Television station in Baltimore, Maryland as a commentator and have written op-ed columns that have appeared in the *Baltimore Sun, The Capital* and expanded to *The Chicago Tribune* newspapers. In each role, activism and civil rights had been the main focus.

Both as an activist and opinion writer, I was fortunate to have had the opportunity to interview famous people and to hear their views on life as African Americans and share my thoughts. I've met notable writers, poets, activists, and talk show hosts such as Oprah Winfrey, James Baldwin, Rosa Parks, Alex Haley, Coretta Scott King, Maya Angelou, Eldridge Cleaver, John Lewis and Nikki Giovanni to name a few.

As a host moderator at WANN radio station, I had interviewed people of various ideologies and religious views including Minister Louis Farrakhan, Reverend Jesse Jackson, Dick Gregory, Stokey Carmichael (Kwame Toure), Congresswoman Maxine Waters, Congresswoman Barbara Jordan, Congressman Parren J. Mitchell and others. What I realized is that they all had a common denominator: they were all activists and like me, had a propensity for social justice causes. Each one in his/her own way instilled within me the strength to move forward toward fighting for justice.

I had discovered that the path toward justice is long, meandering and often difficult but as some would remind me there is a light of justice which shines at the end of the tunnel.

My experiences have shown me a lot over more than 50 years of activism. I've had the dubious distinction of suing the Federal Bureau of Investigation and winning the federal lawsuit against the FBI for surveilling me from ages 15 to 24 years old.

The Federal Bureau of Investigation had an illicit surveillance program known as COINTELPRO, its counterintelligence program. It was a program that spied on people ranging from Malcolm X to Dr. Martin Luther King, Jr. It created dossiers on tens of thousands of U.S. citizens.

The late Alan Hilliard Legum, a prominent Annapolis civil rights lawyer successfully sued the FBI on my behalf and a federal judge awarded me attorney's fees and ordered that the FBI expunge my file. However, before doing so, they gave me hundreds of pages of the dossier that they had maintained.

I, in turn, donated these files to the Maryland chapter of the American Civil Liberties Union, where they placed it on their website so that citizens could read for themselves how the FBI operated in those days. There are many lessons to be learned from the past.

Over the years due to my activism and politics, I have been profiled in newspapers ranging from the Wall Street Journal to the Washington Post. I have experienced first-hand the power of the media.

When I was employed at WJZ-TV in Baltimore, Maryland, I was a panelist on a public affairs program called "Square-Off." Both Oprah Winfrey and I worked at the television station during the same time. This provided me opportunities to speak with her on a number of occasions about various topics. Once, I had her speak at a public housing community called Meade Village located in Severn, Maryland on a topic of self-reliance.

I have served as an elected official in the State of Maryland and as a cabinet member at both the local and state levels of government. My experiences have given me a unique outlook on life.

I often say, "some people watch clocks to tell what time it is, I watch people and I know what time it is."

As a result of my noteworthy observations, a number of years ago Rick Hutzell, editor of the Capital-Gazette newspaper hired me to write bi-weekly columns. My articles have focused on race, racism, poverty, politics, governance and avarice. The Chicago Tribune, which owns the Capital Gazette, also publishes my columns. I received permissions from the Capital and the Chicago Tribune to publish many of these articles.

Over the years, many people have encouraged me to write a book. I decided I would start by sharing with a larger audience my commentaries and observations on local, national and international issues.

As you read the chapters you will find my views on various issues. Some of the readers will agree with the views that are presented here, while others will not.

It was the great Maya Angelou who said, "A bird doesn't sing because it has an answer, it sings because it has a song." I hope that as you read this book, you will find a song to sing.

I want to thank the Trafford Publishing, Inc. and the very patient Sasha Berdin, who worked with me over many months in preparing this book for publication. This book is dedicated to my soulmate who through it all never lost faith.

Enjoy. Share. Stay Woke.

Carl Snowden: Protesters can expect scrutiny

Recently, I was talking to Yevola Peters, a special assistant to Anne Arundel County Executive Steve Schuh. Mrs. Peters, who once headed the Community Action Agency, reminded me of the time she discovered the FBI had created a file on her because of our association.

Mrs. Peters, who was 80 years old, had seen me in my many different roles over the years. At that time, I was the president of the board of directors of the Community Action Agency when she was its executive director. She wondered aloud how I had survived over the years.

As an outspoken critic of the status quo, I have had more than my fair share of criticism and threats and I have seen and felt the force of powerful people, who over the years have sought to silence me for being outspoken.

The truth is that years ago I lost the fear of death. My public career started at age 15; I was deeply influenced by the civil rights movement and the assassinations of President John F. Kennedy, Malcolm X, Martin Luther King Jr. and Sen. Robert F. Kennedy. I knew at an early age that there are consequences for holding views contrary to the mainstream.

I grew up in an era of challenge, change and uncertainty. When many of my peers were going to parties and dances, I was organizing demonstrations.

Few people can imagine what it was like to have the FBI surveil you from ages 15 to 24. Mrs. Peters discovered that because of her association with me, the FBI had created a file on her as well. At that time, I worked for her in the Agency's Youth Development Program.

When I was a student at the Key School, the FBI interviewed my teachers, parents, friends and associates, concluding that I was a "Negro who did not show a propensity for violence."

Thanks to a brilliant lawyer, Alan H. Legum, who successfully sued the FBI on my behalf in 1977, I was able to win both a monetary settlement as well as access to my FBI files.

The late federal District Court Judge Frank Kauffman found that the actions of the government were unconstitutional and that I was a victim of governmental overreach because of my civic activism. He ordered the FBI to destroy my files and pay my attorney's fees.

I was given copies of my FBI files, which I made public and donated to the American Civil Liberties Union of Maryland, which were uploaded on their website. I wanted to make sure people had an opportunity to see how their tax dollars had been spent and what happens when the government begins harassing people for their political views. Anyone interested can call the ACLU at 410-889-8550; it will direct them to its Web page and the Carl Snowden FBI files.

Years later, Republican Anne Arundel County Executive John R. Leopold had the county police create dossiers on me, and his other political opponents. However, when it was later exposed by the press that Mr. Leopold was conducting illicit activities, ironically he was the one arrested and convicted for those actions. During the Leopold controversy a number of years ago, the press focused almost exclusively on Mr. Leopold's sexual proclivities. He later resigned in disgrace. Like President Nixon, he is the only county executive to leave office before his term was completed. Few paid attention to the fact that he was convicted of using the police for political purposes.

Dr. King once said that the greatness of America is the right to protest for right. But he and so many others discovered that protest and protesters are often the victims of government shenanigans.

I have been very fortunate and blessed in many ways. Blessed to have a supportive family and a caring and supportive community. I know that not everyone prays at night for my well-being, but over the course of more than half a century of activism, I have learned something so fundamental and so profound that it has been the reason that I have, despite many political attacks over the years, survived and outlived many of my most powerful critics.

I have learned there is a power in the universe. It is a power that put wetness in water; blue in the sky and allows birds to fly. It is the power that, even today, allows me without fear or equivocation to say, *A Luta Continua*, which in Portuguese means that the struggle continues.

POLITICS

Carl O. Snowden and
U.S. Congressman Parren J. Mitchell

The 1965 Voting Rights Act, which guaranteed the right to vote for African-Americans, became the basis in which I would become an elected official. I was elected to the Annapolis City Council in 1985 at the age of 32.

When I ran for election in a majority African-American ward that was created as a result of a federal voting rights lawsuit brought by Attorney Chris Brown and the American Civil Liberties Union, that successful lawsuit resulted in an increase of African-Americans serving on the City Council.

The ACLU had sued the city based on the fact that in a city with eight wards, which at the time had a 35% African-American population had only one ward represented by an African-American. The federal lawsuit was settled and a new majority-black ward was created.

When I ran for office, I had a number of prominent individuals supporting me. Campaigning for me was the Reverend Jesse Jackson, who in 1984 had run for president; Congressman Parren J. Mitchell, Maryland's first black congressman; and Baltimore City's State's Attorney Kurt Schmoke who later would become that city's first black mayor.

I won the election and served for 12 years before deciding to run for mayor. I lost in a close Democratic primary. However, I was later hired by Governor Parris Glendening and later by County Executive Janet S. Owens, who was the first female elected as county executive in Anne Arundel County, Maryland.

Years later, I would be appointed the first civil rights director for the Office of the Maryland Attorney General by Douglas F. Gansler. The following columns were all written following those experiences.

Carl Snowden: Voting Rights Act changed America

July 14, 2015

This year marks the 50th anniversary of the historic Voting Rights Act. This act, signed by President Lyndon Baines Johnson, forever changed politics in America. Literally thousands of African-Americans, Latinos and others became elected officials because of this law. As the movie "Selma" demonstrated, this right came at a great cost. People gave their lives so that people who previously could not vote had an opportunity to vote.

My mother, who was born in 1917, was born in a society that did not allow women to vote and disenfranchised people of color. Women would win the right to vote in 1920. African-Americans would have that right guaranteed in 1965 by the Voting Rights Act.

In the state of Maryland, the first black elected official would be elected from the city of Annapolis in 1873.Yet, it took a federal Voting Rights Act lawsuit that was filed in 1984 against the City of Annapolis that led to our City Council being more representative of the community that it serves.

Our state did not elect its first African-American congressman until 1971 and did not elect the first black congresswoman until 2008.

In the city of Annapolis, the first African-American alderwoman was elected in 1997. Now, we have two African-American alderwomen serving on this nine-member body.

I have been an eyewitness to history. I have seen so many changes as a result of the Voting Rights Act. I knew the late state Senator Aris T. Allen Sr., the only African-American from our county to serve in the General Assembly. I campaigned for the late Sarah Carter, the only African-American woman to be elected to the Anne Arundel County Council.

Had it not been for the Congress passing this historic legislation, the Voting Rights Act, it is doubtful that the limited progress we have seen in our community would have occurred. Had there been no Voting Rights Act, voters might have never had an opportunity to vote for an Aris Allen, Sarah Carter or a Barack Obama.

Those history-makers may have never held public offices and our city, county, country and world would have been deprived of their leadership, and while some may think that would have been great, the voters thought otherwise.

A Luta Continua, in Portuguese, simply means that the struggle continues!

Carl Snowden: It's time to use the ballot

March 08, 2016

"Give us the ballot," Dr. Martin Luther King Jr. exhorted at a 1957 march on Washington that most Americans are unaware of. They are more familiar with King's famous "I Have a Dream" speech, delivered in 1963.

In some ways the 1957 speech is a better barometer to determine the progress that we have made in race relations and the social justice movement in our nation.

If you lived in Anne Arundel County in 1957, when Dr. King called on America to give us the ballot, you would be living in a jurisdiction that had no African-Americans serving in any countywide elected offices. If you were black, you would be paying taxes and yet would not have an opportunity to elect your representatives.

In fact, in 1957, if you were black, the only high school you could attend was Wiley H. Bates in Annapolis, regardless of what part of the county you lived in.

Too often people do not stop to think about what the legacy of racism has meant and, more specifically, what being denied the ballot has produced. Here are some facts that cannot be ignored:

Only three blacks have ever served on the Anne Arundel County Council: the late Sarah Carter, Daryl Jones and current Councilman Pete Smith.

Only one African-American — the late State Senator Aris T. Allen Sr. — ever served in the General Assembly from Anne Arundel County. He was first elected as a delegate and later appointed to the Senate.

The General Assembly has the dubious distinction in 1909 of passing a grandfather clause that disenfranchised thousands of African-American voters and was reversed only after a 1915 U.S. Supreme Court ruling declared it unconstitutional.

It was a law that said, in effect, that if your grandfather could not vote, neither could you. Just as the U.S. Supreme Court's infamous Dred Scott decision, also written by a Marylander, Chief Judge Roger B. Taney, justified white supremacy, and declared blacks had no rights that whites were bound to respect, the General Assembly stripped blacks of the right to vote.

In the 366-year history of the judiciary, only two African-Americans have served on the Circuit Court in the county: Clayton Greene Jr. and former Judge Rodney C. Warren. The latter was appointed by former Gov. Parris N. Glendening and was later defeated when he ran for election. No black woman has ever served on the Circuit Court in county history.

The late Mary Sellman Jackson was the only African-American to be elected to serve on the county's Orphans Court. These are the facts.

Whenever these facts are stated, some bigoted whites always say that perhaps the black candidates were not "qualified." They conveniently want to overlook a racist system based on the premise of white supremacy.

3

They do not want to be reminded that Alabama Gov. George C. Wallace, then a segregationist, ran for president and won Anne Arundel County each time he ran, including in 1972.

Nor do some whites — including at least one Circuit Court judge — like the fact that there are black legislators and others seeking to remove the statute of Chief Justice Taney from the State House grounds.

In 1957, when Dr. King called on the nation to give us the ballot, little did he know more than 50 years later not a single African-American living in Anne Arundel County would be serving on the county's Circuit Court, school board or General Assembly delegation.

These are the facts, and we are determined to change them.

The Caucus of African-American Leaders hosted a candidates forum for the U.S. Senate, House of Representatives and Circuit Court judgeships.

Dr. King reminded us that in a democracy the greatest march an American can participate in is the march to the ballot box. We now have the ballot. Tonight, that march begins.

A Luta Continua, which means in Portuguese that the struggle continues.

Carl Snowden: Governor Hogan takes right stance on Trump

October 20, 2016

What seems like an eternity will come to an end on Tuesday, Nov. 8, with the election of the next president of the United States of America. Donald Trump — who has been the Don Rickles of politics, having managed to insult women, Latinos, African-Americans, a disabled journalist, Republican officeholders and scores of others — will finally hear from the voters of America.

Mr. Trump's campaign has been an ignominious event for many Americans. It is amazing what you find when you take the time to look at how many Republicans he has attacked personally.

In 2007, he told CNN that President George W. Bush "was probably the worst president in the history of the United States." He called U.S. Sen. Ted Cruz of Texas "lying Ted." He called former Florida Governor Jeb Bush "low energy." And he mocked every other Republican challenger he faced in the primaries.

Without predicting the outcome of the election, I suspect many Americans will follow the lead of Governor Larry Hogan, who has made it clear he will not endorse or vote for Mr. Trump. Governor Hogan's position has angered many right-wing politicians, who believed that he should support the Republican nominee just because he is a Republican.

Governor Hogan has set a standard all elected officials may want to consider: voting for the most qualified candidate regardless of party affiliation, race or gender. Quite frankly, I have been impressed with Governor Hogan's approach to governing.

I know there are those who say Governor Hogan is doing this for political reasons, because he is in a blue state like Maryland that is likely to go for Hillary Clinton anyway. However, when you compare his position to other politicians — including County Executive Steve Schuh and Annapolis Mayor Mike Pantelides, both Republican officials who have endorsed Mr. Trump — you see a sharp contrast in leadership.

Mr. Schuh, when asked at a meeting of the Caucus of African-American Leaders, made it clear that he didn't support many of Mr. Trump's inflammatory and racist comments, but supported his conservative commitment to governance. Mr. Schuh did not win over many in the audience that evening. There is something odd about saying that although someone has offended millions of his fellow Americans, you will endorse and vote for him anyway.

I will never understand how Senator Cruz was able to endorse Donald Trump. Mr. Trump insulted Senator Cruz's wife and inferred that his father was involved in the assassination of President John F. Kennedy.

On the other hand, Governor Hogan took a principled stand, long before other Republican officeholders found the courage to say no to a candidate who is sexist and racist. Mr. Hogan seems to understand what many of other Republican officeholders could not bring themselves to understand: What is good for America will always trump (no pun intended) political expediency.

Like Governor Hogan, I could not support a person for the office of president, who had insulted women, African-Americans, Latinos, and members of the military. The Republican candidate for president never apologized for attacking a Gold Star Muslim family whose son died defending our nation.

Governor Hogan understood that Donald Trump, like Don Rickles, can at times be an amusing comedian, but that he can never be president of the United States of America.

On Nov. 8, Americans will make a decision about who they want to represent them, I will be doing everything I can to make sure that Governor Hogan's position is affirmed by the voters — i.e., no to racism and yes to an America where the commander in chief commands the respect of all Americans, not just the bigots.

Carl Snowden: Broadened participation in voting benefits all

November 08, 2016

Today, millions of Americans are joining in the greatest march that citizens can participate in, the march to the ballot box. By the end of the day, we in this county will have helped select a new president and new U.S. senator, as well as picking members of the Circuit Court. On all three branches of our government — the executive, the legislative and the judicial — we, the people, will have made known our views.

President Barack Obama prudently advised Americans to "not boo, but vote." First lady Michelle Obama advice's was, "When they go low, we go high."

I want to commend a number of people who made it possible for more citizens to participate in our democracy.

House of Delegates Speaker Michael E. Busch and members of the General Assembly enacted early voting, which has proven to be a great success. To see thousands of people lining up at polling places during early voting throughout Anne Arundel County is a great reaffirmation of a system that allows people to express their preferences for candidates, ranging from president to local Board of Education members.

This has not always been the case. Our history is replete with examples of people not being allowed to participate in this great experiment we call democracy. There was a time when women were denied the right to vote. But they won this right in 1920 and now make up more than 53 percent of the electorate.

I am often reminded by my mother, who was born in 1916, that her own mother could not vote, Now she will have an opportunity to cast a ballot for a woman to become president of the United States of America, just as eight years ago she joined with fellow Americans in electing an African-American president.

In 1957, at a Prayer Pilgrimage for Freedom in Washington, D.C., the Rev. Martin Luther King Jr. said, "Give us the ballot." He knew that if all Americans had the right to march, they also had the right to vote. This precious right is why patriots said, "No taxation without representation."

We have learned that every voice should be heard and that the best government is a government that reflects the people it serves. This is why we constantly remind our elected officials of their responsibility to represent all of the people.

We have not reached the zenith of our democracy. We are not a perfect union, yet we are making progress. To see Latinos, Asian-Americans, African-Americans, whites and others who make up the American family exercising their right to vote is indeed special.

I was so proud of the Caucus of African-American Leaders, the District 30 Democratic Club, the NAACP and the clergy as they worked to mobilize citizens to participate in this historic election. A special shout-out goes to Apostle Larry Lee Thomas Sr. and other clergy for their successful "Souls to the Polls" efforts during early voting.

By 8 p.m. today, the polls will be closed. The voters will have spoken.

This year's presidential election has been both contentious and at times dreadful. Yet we will witness what too few nations see: a peaceful transition of power. Regardless of the outcome, Americans will accept the decision of their fellow Americans. This decision will be easier to accept because all Americans will have been allowed to participate in the greatest march ever conceived of: the march to the ballot box.

In many ways, each election is a continuation of our collective efforts to create a better world for unborn generations, which is precisely why I maintain that while we have not reached our goals, we must keep struggling to make America better, not bitter.

A Luta Continua, which in Portuguese means that the struggle continues.

Carl Snowden: Trump showed elections have consequences

April 10, 2017

That elections have consequences is an adage as old as democracy. Over and over, community activists have told people their votes make a difference.

The truth of the adage is becoming painfully clear as issues near and dear to people are suddenly being adversely affected by the Trump administration.

Those concerned about the health of the Chesapeake Bay have seen drastic cuts in federal funding proposed. Those concerned about climate change are seeing the Department of Energy headed by former Texas Gov. Rick Perry, who famously said he wanted to abolish the same agency he is now in charge of.

President Trump said in 2011, that he doesn't believe in global warming: "The science is not settled on this. The idea that we would put Americans' economy at jeopardy based on scientific theory that's not settled yet to me is just nonsense — just because you have a group of scientists who stood up and said here is the fact."

President Donald Trump put Dr. Ben Carson, a former presidential candidate, in charge of the U.S. Department of Housing and Urban Development, which will have a profound impact on residents living in public housing.

Dr. Carson, who admitted he knew nothing about this agency, would have been better suited to be the surgeon general or even the secretary of the Department of Health and Human Services.

All this underscores the importance of people getting involved in elections. Perhaps the silver lining in the clouds from the election of President Trump is that citizens are getting involved.

On a recent Sunday afternoon I attended a town hall meeting on immigration at the First Presbyterian Church in Annapolis. It was jam-packed. Those in attendance included Maryland's U.S. senators, Ben Cardin and Chris Van Hollen; U.S. Rep. Anthony Brown, D-Prince George's; state Sen. Ed Reilly, R-Crofton; and Alderman Kenny Kirby, D-Ward 6. These elected officials had to be impressed not only by the size of the audience but also the passion that was on display.

Elected officials are now seeing an uptick in participation by voters. More people are now attending city and county council meetings than ever before. You can feel the energy from these grass-roots movements on immigration, development, education and issues involving racial justice.

This is healthy for our democracy. An informed and motivated voter is America's best hope. What has pleased me to no end is the people who are now getting involved.

When the women's marches were held earlier this year, the number of participants spoke volumes, but the question was: Can it be sustained? The answer was a resounding "yes."

Federal officials found this out when so many people rallied to save Obamacare that even the most conservative elements of the government knew they could not repeal and replace it with legislation only 17 percent of the nation supported.

Voters are itching to express themselves at the ballot box and are already planning for the mid-term elections next year. But the activists in Anne Arundel County have decided this year's Annapolis elections will be their test for community participation. Although the primary election is not until September, candidates are already knocking on doors and distributing material.

This evening the Caucus of African-American Leaders is meeting from 5 to 8 p.m. at the Wiley H. Bates Legacy Center at 1101 Smithville St. in Annapolis.

Candidates and their supporters are welcome. These meetings are open to the public and I suspect we will have a full house.

The Caucus will be holding candidates forums and doing surveys on issues that impact the community.

In past city elections, getting people to the polls was always a challenge. This time, with so much at stake, it won't be. In part, this is due to President Trump, who has been in office fewer than a hundred days, but has made everyone understand that elections do have consequences.

A Luta Continua, which means, in Portuguese, that the struggle continues.

Carl Snowden: Anne Arundel County Circuit Court membership will change

May 22, 2017

The difference between a "movement" and a "moment" is commitment and sacrifice. A couple of weeks ago scores of protesters stood in front of the Annapolis courthouse on Church Circle in driving rain, protesting the lack of diversity on the Anne Arundel County Circuit Court.

They pointed out that no African-American woman and no Latino or Asian has served on this court in it's 366-year history. Whether the governor was a Democrat or a Republican, whether he was liberal or conservative, black women and other minorities have been excluded from the bench — period.

Just two African-American males have served: Clayton Greene Jr., who is now on the Maryland Court of Appeals, and Rodney C. Warren.

In the county's District Court, the demonstrators noted, the situation is not much better. Four African-Americans have served there: Greene, Essom V. Ricks Jr. and the currently serving Judges Danielle M. Mosley and Shaem C.P. Spencer. Mary Sellman Jackson was the only African-American to ever serve on the county Orphans Court.

It's not as if qualified African-American lawyers have not applied for the Circuit Court. They include Tracey Parker Warren, Keith J. Gross, Gloria Shelton Wilson, Ginina Jackson Stevens, Lorraine Jeanette Rice, Claudia Barber, Kevin Outing, Sheila E. Lundy-Moreau, Evelyn Darden, Doris Walker and Rickey Nelson Jones.

The late state Senator Aris T. Allen Sr. once commented that to be a judge in this county, the law school you attended or your ranking there doesn't matter — you have to have a governor who likes you.

But sometimes whom the voters like is more important. The current Circuit Court has a number of judges who circumvented the process by running successfully against sitting judges. I suspect we'll see this again next year.

The issue won't go away. The protesters at the last demonstration included whites, blacks, Latinos, women, housewives and lawyers. There will be another demonstration in front of the courthouse on June 7. The historic systemic exclusion of people of color is not acceptable.

There is growing progressive movement in Anne Arundel. Groups like Action Annapolis, Huddle, Anne Arundel County/Annapolis Indivisible, Showing Up for Racial Justice and Women Indivisible Strong and Effective are joining forces with the NAACP and the Caucus of African-American Leaders to bring about social change.

Are we going to have our courts and government reflect the people they serve? The demonstrators have taken up that cause. They know there is something wrong with a court system that does not reflect the people that it serves.

There is something wrong when, in 2017, clearly qualified black women are being passed over. Lawyers in this county knows this. Judges know it. Politicians know it.

Moments come and go, movements change things. Governor Larry Hogan had an opportunity to make history with the stroke of a pen by appointing a qualified African-American, Latino or Asian to the Circuit Court. He did not. Like his predecessors, he maintained the status quo.

The growing movement will manifest itself at the ballot box this year in Annapolis and next year in the county. It will move from protest to progress.

History always vindicates those who were right. We now know who was right on slavery, women's rights, the labor movement and civil rights. In our lifetime, we will see African-American women serving on the Circuit Court in Anne Arundel County.

Why? Because the Rev. Martin Luther King Jr. was right when he said, "Truth crushed to the earth will rise again and no lie can live forever."

There are some battles that are worth fighting. One of them is for a society based on diversity, fairness and justice; one that is inclusive and not exclusive.

A Luta Continua, which means in Portuguese that the struggle continues for equality and justice.

Carl Snowden: Know the city candidates' positions on key issues

September 16, 2017

In just three days, Annapolis will hold its primary election to determine the candidates who will advance to the November general election.

If you are like most voters, you probably haven't made up your mind yet. Therefore, it is important to begin to scrutinize the platforms of the candidates and their positions on a host of important issues.

One of the looming issues facing the city is affordable housing. Longtime Annapolitans and their children are being priced out of the real estate market. Firefighters, teachers, police and others in middle-income families are finding it difficult to afford to live in the city.

You can imagine what poor people are going through during this tough downturn in the rental housing market.

If you live in the Morris H. Blum Senior Apartments, you experience elevators breaking down frequently. If you live in Newtowne 20, a public housing community, you know the development needs major renovation.

If you live in subsidized housing in Annapolis, you experience problems that will only be exacerbated by proposed cuts in federal funding that will leave the Housing Authority for the City of Annapolis scrambling for resources to rehabilitate aging housing stock.

There have been recommendations HACA sell the Harbour House apartments in Eastport to private developers and that smaller apartment units be built elsewhere. What is the position of the mayoral and aldermanic candidates on this proposal? How do they propose that the city address this problem?

Crime is another issue. Annapolis experienced its highest homicide rate last year. Is community policing the answer? If so, what is it going to cost taxpayers?

How do you improve police-community relations? The Caucus of African-American Leaders, the local branches of the NAACP and the American Civil Liberties Union recommended the city create a civilian review board for the police. What position do candidates for mayor and City Council have on this proposal?

What about the controversial Crystal Spring project? Should it move forward?

These and dozens of other important questions need to be answered prior to Tuesday's primary.

Campaigns are always about the future. Where is Annapolis headed?

Slick commercials, large yard signs and mailings all tell you who is running. They do not tell you what the candidate will do if elected mayor or a member of the City Council.

There was a time when all candidates had to do was smile, kiss babies and talk about lowering property taxes. Today, we need public officials who will address real systemic problems in our community — problems that if left unattended will only get worse.

When voters go to the polls on Tuesday, they will need to know two things: If I vote for this candidate, will he or she make the quality of life better for me and my family? And who else can I take to the polls with me?

Before you vote, make sure that you know not only who you are voting for, but, what they stand for.

Carl Snowden: Like all elections, that in Annapolis is a referendum on incumbents

October 24, 2017

The most important march in which an American can participate in a democracy is the march to the ballot box. In just 14 days Annapolitans will be able to cast their ballots in the city's general election. Every election is about the future and serves as a referendum on the incumbents.

If you like the direction in which the city is heading, you will vote to maintain the status quo. If not, you will vote for change.

I am voting for change. There are things that have happened over the last four years that bother me.

It was troublesome to see our city experience the highest homicide rate in its history. It was disturbing to see families in mourning and communities looking for empathy receive neither empathy nor sympathy. Most of the victims of these homicides were not household names, but many were native Annapolitans.

I thought about the role previous mayors played during times of challenge and sadness. I remember seeing mayors attend the funerals of victims. I remember how they gave words of comfort to grieving families and distressed communities. Regardless of their party affiliation, they came to offer their condolences.

I remember attending a funeral at Mount Moriah AME Church with then-Mayor Al Hopkins. I remember him comforting the family of the deceased, a person he did not personally know. Yet, he knew that his role as mayor was to show empathy to this grieving family.

Mayor Roger W. "Pip" Moyer Sr. would always be at the funeral of an Annapolitan. He didn't do so to be a big shot. He demonstrated a genuine concern for all Annapolitans. When he left public office, he would still attend the funerals of his constituents.

Our current mayor, Michael Pantelides, did not attend any of the funerals of the murdered victims. Neither did he attend the funeral of the late Annapolis police Detective Shelly C. White Sr., who served this community honorably for 19 years and who had claimed that he was the victim of racial discrimination. When he died suddenly, his funeral was attended by hundreds.

Personnel from the Naval Academy were present. Members of the Anne Arundel County Police Department were part of an honor guard. Community leaders from Bywater, Robinwood, Newtowne 20 and the Morris H. Blum apartments were there.

Yet conspicuously absent were Mayor Mike Pantelides, then-Police Chief Michael Pristoop and other elected officials. Why were they missing? Why didn't they lower the city's flag for this man who served this community?

Elections are referendums on incumbents and they should be.

I thought about the crude language President Donald Trump used to insult NFL players because he disagreed with their kneeling in protest of controversial police shootings. Then I thought of Mayor Pantelides' "call off the dogs" comment directed at Robert Eades and William Rowel.

Both comments by chief executive officers reflected badly on these public servants.

In America, the beauty of this democracy is that every voter is equal. The vote of the millionaire is no greater than the vote of someone who is unemployed.

Two weeks from today, all eligible city voters will have an opportunity to cast their ballots. Some undoubtedly will vote for the status quo. But I will use the standard famously posed by President Ronald Reagan, who asked voters, "Are you better off than you were four years ago?"

Every voter will have a response to that question and in just 14 days we will know the answer.

A Luta Continua, which in Portuguese means that the struggle continues!

Carl Snowden: City makes progress toward diversity, inclusiveness

November 14, 2017

Every campaign has winners and losers, and last week's mayoral election was no exception. The winners included the Latino community, which saw Democratic Ward 5 candidate Marc Rodriguez become the first Latino elected to the Annapolis City Council.

He will not be the last. As the city's demographics change, so will the political complexion of the City Council. The next City Council will have three African-American women and a Latino.

Representative government is a good thing. I am always reminded of the joke former U.S. Sen. Barbara A. Mikulski would tell: "You either have a seat at the table or you are on the menu."

In so many ways, people of color have wanted a seat at the table — an opportunity to give their perspectives on the issues facing our city, county, state, and nation.

The Caucus of African-American Leaders became actively involved in this year's city campaign, endorsing eight of the nine eventual winners. The caucus wanted to make sure it had a seat at the table — and we do.

Mayor-elect Gavin Buckley, candidates and elected officials have joined the caucus and have been coming for years to our monthly meeting. They got to know us and we got to know them. We enthusiastically endorse them and our only request was that our government reflect the people that it serves.

As Mayor-elect Buckley prepares his transition team, we are confident we will have a seat at the table. We believe that when everyone is at the table, the diversity of ideas that emerges helps all citizens.

When the Caucus of African-American Leaders first advocated that police officers be required to wear body cameras, there was some resistance. Today both the police and the citizens applaud our efforts.

As the mayor-elect begins the process of selecting department heads and members of his staff, we will see the change that voters wanted. We will see an inclusionary administration.

I have had the privilege of serving in government in many capacities. I was an elected official in the city and a member of the Cabinet of then-County Executive Janet S. Owens. I was appointed by then-state Attorney General Douglas F. Gansler as the first director of civil rights in the Office of the Attorney General.

In these roles, I learned that what voters and citizens want is a government that reflects their values.

They want to make sure that those who lead us understand what it is to be a public servant. They want officials who will return our calls, listen to our needs and not abuse the trust that we have placed in them.

As a result of last week's election, we have a new mayor-elect, a new first lady, Julie Wiliams Buckley, and an opportunity to make Annapolis a city that celebrates its diversity and honors its history.

We believe that when everyone has a seat at the table, the menu will be decided by those who are seated.

Carl Snowden: In this year's election voters will look for change

April 09, 2018

The upcoming midterm elections will offer voters an opportunity to send a message.

President Ronald Reagan once observed that if voters liked the last four years, they should vote for the status quo. What we are witnessing is that voters do not seem to like the status quo. In one special election after another, voters are voting for change.

We saw this last year in the red state of Alabama, where a Democrat was elected to fill the U.S. Senate seat that had been held by U.S. Attorney General Jeff Sessions. We saw the same thing in our neighboring purple state of Virginia, in which Democrats made significant gains.

Closer to home, during last year's municipal election in Annapolis, Democrats won the mayoral election and seven of the eight aldermanic elections. Among the latter, only Republican Alderman Fred Paone managed to hold on to his seat in a very closely contested race.

The question that must be asked now: Will these local elections bring real change? Mayor Gavin Buckley has said the answer is yes.

We are already seeing change. Mayor Buckley's fledgling administration has now brought in a new city manager, city attorney and chief of staff — and, with those changes, a lot of expectations.

Many of us are assuming that we should see less litigation and more mediation, less police and community confrontation and more cooperation.

In just a few short months, Mayor Buckley has now has appointed a majority of the board of commissioners of the Housing Authority for the City of Annapolis. In part, this came about because of the resignations of previous appointees. Will there be an improvement in the quality of life of the residents of properties overseen by the Housing Authority? Will we see a reduction in poverty and crime? These questions and others will surely be answered soon.

When voters go to the polls for the primary elections for county, state and congressional positions, I am sure they will carefully examine the people who are running. They want to know who is running and why.

Unlike past elections, where there was a notable drop-off in interest as voters went down the ballot, in this primary enlightened voters will review the candidates for every office, from governor to judge of the Orphans' Court.

This evening at 5, for the monthly meeting of the Caucus of African-American Leaders, we have invited candidates to meet and greet the voters. Our meetings are at the Wiley H. Bates Legacy Center at 1101 Smithville St. in Annapolis and are open to the public. We provide a complimentary dinner and beverage and an opportunity for candidates to talk with potential constituents.

Mayor Buckley attended these meetings before being elected, as did many members of the City Council. They had an opportunity to hear what was on the minds of voters. It paid off.

19

I suspect candidates for Congress, governor, lieutenant governor, comptroller, county executive, state Senate, House of Delegates, sheriff, judge and other offices will want to stop by and meet empowered, educated, involved voters.

These voters not only have great hopes for the future but have proven they will vote accordingly if they believe their interests are threatened. The voters who attend these meetings are likely to quote former U.S. Rep. William Clay of St. Louis, who said that in politics "there are no permanent enemies, and no permanent friends, only permanent interests."

A Luta Continua, which means in Portuguese that the struggle continues.

Carl Snowden: City residents need to cast informed votes

July 23, 2018

This summer in Annapolis, candidates will be knocking on your doors and you will receive numerous solicitations for your vote by mail, robocalls, sign-waving, yard signs and a host of rallies and community meetings.

Elections are a referendum on the performance of elected officials. As Annapolis gears up for its September primary, a slew of candidates have announced they are running for office. There are contests in both the Republican and Democratic mayoral primaries. Voters this summer and fall will have an opportunity to evaluate the performance of all of the incumbents and the promises of the challengers.

As a native Annapolitan, I know how unpredictable local races can be. Over the years, I have seen well-funded candidates lose and candidates on shoe-string budgets emerge as winners.

I fondly remember the election of former Alderwoman Cynthia Abney Carter, the first African-American woman elected to the City Council. Her candidacy defied the odds: She was a write-in candidate and the political pundits dismissed her. Yet she won, and this became the catalyst for other successful underdog campaigns. One was that of Alfred A. Hopkins, who defeated incumbent Mayor Dennis Callahan in spite of being outspent 10-to-1.

As a former three-term member of the City Council and a mayoral candidate, I have advised scores of candidates over the years. My advice is always the same: No one is invincible. Never assume any candidate is an automatic winner. If you work hard and find issues that resonate with voters, it makes a big difference.

Numerous groups — including the NAACP, Action Annapolis, the Sierra Club and the Caucus of African-American Leaders — are working full-time to publicize the records of the incumbents and the promises of the challengers.

With so many candidates running, how does the average voter determine who the best candidates are?

First, don't pay attention to slick ads and endorsements. Concentrate on what a candidate has done as an incumbent and what the challengers have done by way of community service. Have they been active in the community? Are they involved in the PTA? Do they spend time with the people they want to represent?

When candidates come knocking at your door over the next few months, seeking your vote, I recommend you ask each of them:

- "If I vote for you, how will the quality of life in my community be improved?"
- "What will you accomplish in your first term?"

Candidates unable to answer these questions do not deserve your vote.

In a democracy, there is nothing more powerful than an informed electorate. Take the time to learn about the position of candidates before you cast your vote. What are their stances on jobs, crime, taxes, recreation, development and affordable housing? Will they commit to supporting having an inclusive government?

My mom, who is 101 years old, understood what the Rev. Martin Luther King Jr. meant when he declared that in a democracy, the greatest march an American can participate in is the march to the ballot box.

We need people marching there in great numbers in September and November. We must remember that elections have consequences.

This year, I am convinced Annapolitans will be paying close attention. I am equally convinced that the 2017 elections will be a dress rehearsal for the 2018 mid-term elections.

One of America's great attributes is that in every election we, the voters, get to remind public servants that they work for us. We have an opportunity to hire and to fire them. So remember, when they ask for your vote, paraphrase President John F. Kennedy: Ask not what my vote can do for you, but what will you do to earn my vote.

A Luta Continua, which means in Portuguese that "the struggle continues."

Carl Snowden: 2018 election results brought many changes to Anne Arundel

November 27, 2018

The recent midterm elections produced a record number of women and African-Americans being elected to public office. Several victories produced historic outcomes. District 32 delegates-elect Mike Rogers and Sandy Bartlett are the first African-Americans to be elected to the Maryland General Assembly from that district. Del. Pam Beidle was elected to the state Senate seat from this district.

The late District 30 Republican State Senator Aris T. Allen, Sr., had been the only African-American elected from the county prior to that. Delegate-elect Bartlett is a lawyer and the only African-American female elected to the General Assembly from this county. Hopefully, this will not be the case in the future.

Another African-American female lawyer was also elected to the Anne Arundel County Orphans court. Judge-elect Vickie Gipson who garnered more than 100,000 votes ousted a Republican incumbent.

Her victory makes her only the second African-American to serve on this court. The late Judge Mary Sellman Jackson was the other African-American. Appeals Court Judge Clayton Greene, Jr, and Judge-elect Gipson are the only elected African-American judges in our county.

In the June Democratic Primary, Democrats elected among others Christine Davenport, Thea Boykins-Wilson, Robert Haynes and Andrea Jones Horton to the Anne Arundel County Democratic Central Committee. These African-Americans were politically savvy and attractive candidates.

The Central Committees have long been the training ground for future candidates. You will undoubtedly see them on future ballots. Daryl Jones, a prominent lawyer was elected twice to the Anne Arundel County Council after being elected to the Democratic Central Committee.

On another note, his successor Councilman Pete Smith will not be returning to the County Council and just as four years ago there was an all-male County Council, when the new County Council is sworn in there will be no African-American's on it.

In the City of Annapolis for the first time in almost 100 years, its City Council has no African-American male serving, after former Alderman Kenneth Kirby decided not to run for reelection.

Regular readers of this column know that the General Assembly disenfranchised black voters in 1909 and it took the U.S Supreme Court to strike down a law passed by the legislature in order to restore African-Americans right to vote.

Even after the Supreme Court struck it down as unconstitutional in 1915, the first black woman, former Alderwoman Cynthia Abney Carter was not elected to the City Council until 1997.

I have long advocated that in a democracy, it is important that the government reflects all of the people that it serves. The Founding Fathers of this nation went to war over the principle of "no taxation without representation." It is an enduring principle. All taxpayers should be represented in policy-making and taxing authority bodies.

I was pleased that voters elected Candice C.W. Antwine to the Board of Education. Given the ongoing controversy involving racist activities in our schools, Antwine will bring an important perspective to that policy-making board along with newly elected board members Melissa Ellis and Dana Schallheim.

The Caucus of African-American Leaders was very involved in this past election. The successful candidates that we endorsed included County Executive-elect Steuart Pittman, State's Attorney-elect Anne Colt Leitess, Clerk of the Court Scott Poyer, District 30 state Senator-elect Sarah Elfreth, Speaker Mike Busch, Delegate-elect Alice Cain, District 33; Delegate-elect Heather Bagnall, Councilwoman-elect Sarah Lacey, Councilman Andrew Pruski, Councilwoman-elect Allison Pickard and Councilwoman-elect Lisa Rodvien among others.

What I think members of our community liked about the candidates that we endorsed was that they didn't just show up at election time. Many of them attended our meetings and churches prior to the election and joined the Caucus and became active members.

The voters have given a mandate to these newly elected officials. They wanted change. They wanted a government that reflected all of the people that it serves.

Very shortly, we will see who gets appointed to policy making positions. Paraphrasing former U.S. Sen. Barbara A. Mikulski, "you either have a seat at the table or you may be on the menu."

Carl Snowden: History repeats itself in Annapolis Ward 6 election

July 09, 2019

History has a way of repeating itself. Last week, DaJuan Gay, 22 won the Ward 6 special election as a write-in candidate.

The same year he was born, in the same Ward 6, Cynthia Abney Carter won a write-in campaign becoming the first African-American woman to serve on the Annapolis City Council.

The successful election of Alderman-elect Gay also fills another void on the City Council, his election means that a black male will now be on the City Council.

When Alderman Kenny Kirby retired, there was no African-American male on the nine-member City Council.

Government works best when we have diversity and elected officials who reflect the makeup of the community that they serve.

The newly elected alderman had the support of County Executive Steuart Pittman, Mayor Gavin Buckley, Kirby — all Democrats — and the Caucus of African-American Leaders.

Gay will finish out the term of Del. Shaneka Henson, who too made history, by becoming the first African-American woman to serve in the Maryland General Assembly representing District 30, which includes the City of Annapolis.

She was appointed to the General Assembly to finished out the term of the late Speaker Michael. Busch.

Gay's election coincided with the homicide of Elijah Mekhi Wilson, 16, of Annapolis who was fatally shot in Ward 6 the day before the special election.

Crime was one of the major issues of that campaign and the death of this teenager was a poignant reminder that this ward needs effective leadership.

Ward 6, which has the largest concentration of public and subsidized housing in the city, certainly will need the energy and attention that the newly elected alderman is expected to bring to the City Council.

Currently, there is a federal lawsuit pending against the City of Annapolis and the Housing Authority for the City of Annapolis alleging racial discrimination. The lawsuit includes residents from Ward 6, including Gay's mother and brother as plaintiffs.

Safe and affordable housing remains a major concern, Gay is expected to play a prominent role in addressing this issue.

The Caucus of African-American Leaders will celebrate the victory of Alderman-elect Gay.

The Caucus will also honor Annapolis police Detective Shomar Johnson, who is accredited with apprehending the alleged killer of Edward Seay, a popular Annapolis rapper aka Tre Da Kid.

Every generation must produce its own leaders to address the societal problems of their era. Last week Ward 6 voters ushered in a new leader. With the help of Lyn Farrow and scores of other volunteers, Gay made history.

His election made us all proud and proved once again the power of the vote. Voting can and does make a difference.

One of the biggest winners were people whose names did not appear on the ballot, i.e., people living in public housing.

They now have a young voice that can speak to their needs and concerns. We join with many Annapolitans in wishing him the best.

He will learn quickly what his predecessors learned that running for public office is easier than governing.

We congratulate him and his team on their impressive victory and remind him of the Portuguese saying, *A Luta Continua*, which means that the struggle continues.

Alderman Gay, now, it's time to roll up your sleeves and go to work. The citizens and voters of Ward 6 have given you a mandate, use it wisely.

Carl Snowden: Recent march displayed new generation of leadership

November 11, 2019

Alderman Kenny Kirby looked at Da'Juan Gay, 19, a sophomore at the University of Maryland, Eastern Shore, who had just announced at the Caucus of African-American Leaders' regular monthly meeting that he was organizing a march in Annapolis to protest the deaths of unarmed African-American men.

Alderman Kirby said, "He is going to be a leader." Alderman Kirby's sentiments are widely shared by a number of political observers and pundits.

Not only was Mr. Gay able to organize, mobilize and energize hundreds of people to participate in the march, it did not go unnoticed that he was able to get whites, blacks, Latinos and other agents for social change to participate.

The march consisted of high school students as well as collegians. They were enthusiasts and idealists. Whites carried placards that read "Black Lives Matter" and an African-American man, Kalemba Kola-Peba, held a sign that read "Black, White, Blue —All Lives Matter."

It was a march reminiscent of another era – an era, in which blacks and whites marched together for social justice. What made this march different from other demonstrations was the number of young people who participated.

They effectively got the word out using social media. They posted on Facebook and Instagram.

I was impressed by the sincerity of these marchers. As they paraded down Main Street, onlookers applauded and some joined in. Some of the marchers sung, "Ain't Gonna Let Nobody Turn Me Around" and others chanted "No Justice, No Peace."

When they reached City Dock, they discussed social inequality. And in the background the expensive sailboats and powerboats quietly passed by.

Cynics have often said that the current generation is not interested in social justice issues. The March for Solidarity proved them wrong.

At a subsequent meeting at City Hall, in which many of these young people eloquently expressed themselves, I advised these young people to hold their elected officials accountable.

I told them to remember that you can bring about change not only by marching but also by voting for candidates who share your vision.

I am sure that, as these young people spoke, there were members of the Annapolis City Council who recognized not only were they up-and-coming leaders, but they were potential contenders for their seats. And that is a good thing!

Every generation has a responsibility to produce new leaders. Alderman Kirby got it right: They are going to be the new leaders. I for one, look forward to their leadership.

A Luta Continua, which in Portuguese means that the struggle continues!

RACISM & DISCRIMINATION

Carl O. Snowden and
American Journalist Jonathan T. Capehart

America's original sin was slavery. Today we see its effects in numerous ways. Poverty, drugs, an unjust criminal justice system and the lack of affordable housing and healthcare.

There are so many examples of racism that no one book could ever contain them all. However, what is clear is that it has a corrosive impact on our society. I see it daily. The hopelessness and despair it produces can be seen in every urban city.

There are areas of America that many Americans have never visited. The "other America" as Dr. Martin Luther King, Jr. called it is an America that cannot coexist with American values.

Racial discrimination in America will literally decide your zip code; the level of education your children will receive; the quality of their healthcare and their expected mortality rate. In the following chapter, I attempt to give the reader a sense of that America.

Carl Snowden: Why Ferguson, NYC incidents matter

December 14, 2014

Why are so many people demonstrating about alleged police misconduct in America today? Why is it that the deaths of Eric Garner and Michael Brown have Americans questioning our criminal justice system?

Although the cases that have gotten the most attention involve African-Americans, this is truly not a black and white issue. It is a moral issue.

It is a right versus wrong issue. Justice versus injustice. One of the underpinnings of the demonstrations that are occurring in America today is that they are multiracial. Americans of various racial backgrounds are questioning whether our criminal justice system is fair.

Americans have been told that "justice is indivisible." Yet, we have witnessed over and over again a system that seems to discriminate based on race, caste, class and color.

There are very few Americans left who do not believe that there is a systemic problem in the criminal justice system.

In case you happen to be one of those Americans, I strongly recommend that you read Michelle Alexander's book, "The New Jim Crow," which documents and substantiates this issue very clearly.

I am fully aware that this column will generate anonymous and hateful comments. Those comments will range from "blacks are criminals" to "Carl Snowden, go back to Africa." The times that we are living in are perilous.

Yet Americans must hear the cries of those who say "Black lives matter," "Hands up," "No justice, no peace."

In Anne Arundel County, we too have had our share of controversial decisions by a judicial system that seems to be oblivious to our concerns.

As a native of this county, I remember cases that have resulted in demonstrations and pleas for justice.

In 2014, demonstrators called on the U.S. Department of Justice to investigate the death of Kendall Green, who was fatally shot after being called a racial slur.

In 2008, demonstrators called on the Department of Justice to investigate the death of Noah Jamahl Jones, who died violently during a racial melee in Pasadena.

I remember receiving a letter from U.S. Sen. Barbara A. Mikulski at the time in which she stated, "The death of this young man was a huge loss to the family and the community. The decision to close the civil rights investigation and hold no one accountable for his death is a travesty."

Indeed, that is what the demonstrations today are about: "travesty" and "accountability." It is a travesty that you can be choked to death on videotape and no one is held accountable.

It is a travesty that Trayvon Martin can die literally blocks from his home and no one is held accountable.

Next year will mark my 45th anniversary as an activist in this state. In those five decades, I have become a grandfather of three. I have raised two sons. I have seen America at its best and at its worst.

I have long understood the need for a persistent and consistent commitment for social justice, coupled with a belief that our actions could make a difference, which is why, even today, I still believe that we can make America a better nation.

I believe that "truth crushed to the earth will rise again." I believe that those demonstrators — black, white and Latino — believe that they can and will change the system and that our best days are ahead of us.

I pray and hope that they are right.

Information is power. Justice is indivisible. Truth is revealing and freedom must never be abandoned. *A Luta Continua*, which means that the struggle for freedom, justice and equality for all people continues.

Carl Snowden: Breakfast served with biscuits, bacon and bigotry

July 28, 2015

Recently, I was at a local diner having breakfast with a friend. We often break bread together, discuss current events and talk about our grandchildren.

On network television that morning was a news story regarding the Republican presidential campaign of Donald Trump. Mr. Trump was loudly proclaiming his opposition to "illegal immigration." He was saying that the Mexican government was sending drug dealers, rapists, prostitutes and every other type of criminal across the border.

Some people watch clocks, I watch people. As Mr. Trump's incendiary assertions were being played in this local restaurant, I observed how people were reacting.

In the dining room was a Latino family, including children. The older adults of that party seemed to be uncomfortable.

Next to their table and mine were some white men having breakfast. They were sharing their views on Mr. Trump and wanted to make sure everyone heard them.

One said, "These people are ruining our country. They are taking our jobs."

Another said, "Earlier this year, the Anne Arundel County Public Schools sent us a notice in English and Spanish."

He and his colleagues went on to lament that "these people" need to learn English and they hated seeing things in Spanish.

"This is our country, and these people need to learn to speak English," said still another.

As I listened to these bigots, I immediately thought about how African-Americans were often the targets of bigots during the desegregation of schools and communities.

I remember the comments: How blacks were "ruining" their schools and communities. That it was the "blacks" who were committing crimes. It was the "blacks" who were the drug dealers and the rapists.

Bigots are consistent in their ignorance and their arrogance. I have seen this movie before.

Since the patrons next to our table were oblivious to the fact that their conversation was interrupting other diners, I decided this would be a "teachable" moment.

I indicated to my fellow diners that I wonder what Native Americans thought when people "illegally" entered their nation.

I said, "You know, when the Pilgrims came to America, it was occupied by people of color. They happen to be the original settlers of the land. They had various native tribes."

I then went on to share my own experiences with Latinos. I have Latino neighbors and my granddaughter goes to Tyler Heights Elementary School, where she has Latino friends who have taught her Spanish words and she has taught them African-American songs.

My Latino neighbors are hardworking Americans who every day get up and go to work. Some work in restaurants or as landscapers, taxicab drivers, maids or health care providers. Some own their own businesses.

Then I decided to underscore a basic belief of mine: Most Americans are from immigrant families. Many of their ancestors came here "illegally," despite their claim that they "discovered" America.

It is my assertion that whether our ancestors came by a slave ship or on Christopher Columbus' Santa Maria, Pinta or Nina, we are all in the same boat now.

America is a nation of immigrants. I have had the pleasure and privilege of traveling abroad and believe me there is no nation in the world like America. This is the most diverse nation in the world.

It is the only nation that is attempting to form a more perfect union. It is the nation that proclaims liberty and justice for all.

Also, it is the one nation where you can have biscuits and bacon for breakfast and be introduced to both bigotry and history at the same time.

I got a broad smile from the Latino family when they were leaving and a frown from some of my fellow criticaster diners, who did not realize that their ancestors were "illegal immigrants."

A Luta Continua, which in Portuguese means the struggle continues!

Carl Snowden: Government must reflect the people it serves

October 06, 2015

Is there "systemic racism" in the Annapolis Police Department? Was the provocative press release question asked by civil rights groups recently?

On Wednesday, at 7 p.m., a public hearing at City Hall being sponsored by the Anne Arundel County branch of the National Association for the Advancement of Colored People, the American Civil Liberties Union and the Caucus of African-American Leaders will be held.

The purpose of this hearing is to give citizens an opportunity to express their views. The hearing will be chaired by William Rowel and panel members will include former alderwoman Classie G. Hoyle, Amy Cruice of the ACLU, and the Rev. Stephen A. Tillett, president of Anne Arundel County NAACP.

Former and current police officers are expected to testify. Efforts are being undertaken to insure that there is no retaliation on police officers currently serving.

In an effort at full disclosure, I am a life member of the both the NAACP, ACLU and a founding member of the Caucus of African-American Leaders.

However, the views, that I am expressing in this column, do not necessarily reflect the views of those organizations. They are my own views.

My opinion is based on a very simple, yet, profound proposition: government ought to reflect the people, that it serves. There is a reason why government workers are called, "public servants." These government workers' salaries and benefits are paid by taxpayers.

Sometimes even our elected officials forget, that they are hired and can be fired by the voters. They too are public servants. The money that they manage are the taxpayers.

In 1776, an oppressed people used the rallying cry, "no taxation without representation" and demanded change.

Today, taxpayers and voters are making it clear, that they do not want their tax dollars to subsidize systemic racism in any form.

As a former three-term member of the Annapolis City Council, I am well aware of the importance of making sure that taxpayers dollars are not used in a discriminatory fashion.

Before people scream that there is no "systemic racism" in Annapolis, the facts, do not support that argument. The Annapolis Police Department was founded in 1867, the first African-American police officers were not hired until 1960 and even then, they were not permitted to arrest whites!

In the 1980s prominent Annapolis civil rights lawyer Alan H. Legum, representing African-American firefighters and police officers, filed successful lawsuits that resulted in federal judges issuing consent decrees requiring that the city's fire and police departments to reflect the citizens they serve.

Again, in the 1980s the U.S. Department of Housing and Urban Development issued findings that the city of Annapolis discriminated against African-Americans through its Urban Renewal and Section 8 programs.

A successful federal Voting Rights lawsuit was filed by the ACLU, which increased the number of African-Americans serving on the City Council. The first African-American woman elected in 1997 to the City Council was former alderwoman Cynthia Abney Carter. These are the facts.

What many Americans are unaware of is that under Title VI of the 1964 Civil Rights Act, local jurisdictions that intentionally discriminate can lose their federal funding.

The proposition that government should reflect the people that it serves and that public dollars, should not be used in a discriminatory manner, is supported both by law and history.

In 1963, President John F. Kennedy said, "Simple justice requires that public funds, to which all taxpayers of all races contribute, not be spent in any fashion which encourages, entrenches, subsidizes or results in racial discrimination"

Malcolm X was far more blunt, "America must practice what it preach or preach what it practice."

In Annapolis, many of us feel that it is time for Annapolis and Anne Arundel County governments to reflect the people that it serves.

Somehow the cry of "taxation without representation" have taken on a social justice quality, that I welcome.

A Luta Continua, which in Portuguese means, that the struggle continues!

Carl Snowden: Why are black judges so scarce?

December 15, 2015

"Why?" is probably the most profound question anyone can ask. Yet, when it comes to racism, people will get angry if the question is raised.

Last month an Anne Arundel County African-American lawyer by the name of Rickey Nelson Jones filed a lawsuit in a Baltimore federal District Court raising the question of "Why?"

Why has there only been two African-Americans – Judges Clayton Greene Jr. and Rodney C. Warren – serving on the Anne Arundel County Circuit Court in 365 years? Why has there never been an African-American woman serving on the court? Why has there never been an Asian or Latino appointed to the bench? Why?

The lawsuit Mr. Jones filed probably will not get those questions answered. I am sure the Maryland judiciary will file motions and ask the federal judge to dismiss the case. Yet, Mr. Jones lawsuit raises some very disturbing questions.

In the past, the judiciary's Trial Court Judge Nominating Commission could make the argument that no qualified African-American or other minority had applied for the position. Not any longer.

As Mr. Nelson' lawsuit indicated, there has been many qualified applicants, including Tracey Parker Warren, an administrative law judge, and Gloria Selena Wilson Shelton, a former assistant state attorney general, who recently applied. Previous African-American applicants have included Keith J. Gross, a graduate of the Naval Academy, Ginina Jackson Stevens, a former assistant public defender, and Kevin Outing and Doris Walker,

Candidates for judge must be 30 years old at the time of appointment. A member of the Maryland bar, and U.S. citizen registered to vote in state elections. Also, they must reside in the county from which they are appointed for at least six-months.

Something is wrong when a criminal justice system does not reflect the people it serves. African-Americans are conspicuously absent from the county's State's Attorney' Office and Office of Law.

Several years ago, the Caucus of African-American Leaders and the Anne Arundel County branch of the NAACP raised questions about the lack of minority representation in these offices. Officials immediately said they would not "lower" their standards or support "quotas" –inflammatory statements designed to put civil rights advocates on the defensive and distract from the issue at hand.

Can you imagine a criminal justice system that excluded whites? Imagine going to court: The bailiff is African-American. The deputy sheriffs are black. The judges, lawyers and juries are all black, and the only white person in the courtroom is the defendant.

White people would not accept such a system. Yet when African-Americans raise the question of why there are no African-American judges, or so few black state's attorneys or court officials, they are accused of playing the "race card."

I am aware this column will bring the bigots out of their closets. I am sure I will receive hate mail and comments not fit for a family newspaper. However, nowhere in their venomous comments will they answer the question "Why?'

I have served in many capacities over my career. I served 12 years on the Annapolis City Council, eight years in the Cabinet of the county executive and six years as the director of civil rights for the Office of the Maryland Attorney General and I have discovered, that the most disturbing question you can ask government officials is "Why?"

The Rev. Martin Luther King Jr. once said, "There comes a time when one must take a position that is neither safe, nor politic, nor popular, but he must take it because conscience tells him it is right".

I want to publicly thank Rickey Nelson Jones for raising the question of why there have been so few African-Americans who have served on the county Circuit Court and I want him to know that as long as there is breath in my body, I intend to make sure the questions he raised in his lawsuit are answered.

A Luta Continua, which in Portuguese means that the struggle continues!

Carl Snowden: We must speak out against Trump

December 22, 2015

Donald Trump has dominated the news for months now. He has become the Don Rickles of politics. He has managed to insult everyone except the racists and the bigots.

He has demeaned women, made fun of the disabled, threatened to break up undocumented Latino families and attacked Muslims, all in a single day!

A billionaire bigot, Trump probably demonstrates what "privilege" in America means better than anyone. His recent announcement that the United States of America should bar any Muslim from entering it and that a databank should be developed to keep track of Muslims should be met with moral outrage and righteous indignation by every American, including members of the Republican Party.

Here is a fact: If the Republican Party, which now controls both chambers of Congress, really wanted to let the world know that it finds Trump's remarks reprehensible, it could introduce and pass a resolution in both legislative bodies officially condemning him for his religious bigotry. But it will not.

Republicans are faced with a dilemma. Donald Trump has hinted – in spite of his most recent pledges — that if the Republican Party treats him "unfairly," he will run as an independent, potentially spoiling the GOP's opportunity to recapture the White House in 2016.

The policies Trump is promoting and espousing border on being fascist and racist. We have seen this before. Demagogues like the late Alabama Gov. George C. Wallace rode racially divisive politics into the governor's mansion. Wallace even managed to win the Democratic primary in Maryland when he ran for president on an anti-busing platform in 1972.

Yes, we have seen these boisterous leaders before. During the Nazi era, there was an outspoken Protestant pastor by the name of Martin Niemoller, who was placed in concentration camps.

He said the following words, which every human being should be required to remember:

"First they came for the socialists, and I did not speak out — because I was not a socialist. Then they came for the trade unionists, and I did not speak out — because I was not a trade unionist. Then they came for the Jews, and I did not speak out — because I was not a Jew. Then they came for me — and there was no one left to speak for me."

That captures well what happens when people remain silent when other people are suffering. Think how many people have remained silent in the face of Donald Trump's blatant bigotry.

I remember so well James Baldwin's open letter to Angela Davis, who was in prison at the time, fighting for her life. He wrote:

"If we know, then we must fight for your life as though it were our own — which it is — and render impassable with our bodies in the corridor to the gas chamber. For, if they take you in the morning, they will be coming for us that night."

James Baldwin and Martin Niemoller knew what I know: When you fail to speak out against hate, it is just a matter of time before your turn comes and there is no one in "the corridor."

We either learn lessons from history or we are doomed to repeat that history. This is why we must continue to struggle for a society that is based on brotherhood, sisterhood and peace.

There was another man, born in a stable, who advocated the same thing and we will be celebrating his birthday in three days. Merry Christmas and Happy Kwanzaa.

A Luta Continua, which means in Portuguese that the struggle continues!

Carl Snowden: Schools need to prevent disturbing incidents

July 28, 2016

On April 16 The Capital published a blaring headline, "School investigating racial epithet written in North County High bathroom."

Readers of this column will recall that this incident came on the heels of a controversial satirical essay written by a white high school student calling for the nuclear annihilation of African-Americans. The student wrote that the nuclear weapon should be used to "wipe the cesspool of filth some call 'race' from the earth." The student, I am told, received an A for his essay.

The controversial essay drew national coverage and raised issues regarding free speech and academic freedom. It also inflamed students and parents, who were outraged.

Can you imagine what the reaction would be if a satirical student essay had called for the elimination of Jews via gas chambers? Even Donald Trump would be hard pressed to find the satirical humor in that essay.

A town hall meeting sponsored by the local NAACP and the Caucus of African-American Leaders in the Humphrey community drew angry and concerned participants. Black students complained that they were being subjected to disparate treatment. They cited examples involving discipline and even the grading of their papers as examples.

This is not a new concern. In fact, the NAACP filed a formal racial discrimination complaint against the county school system with the U.S. Department of Education's Office of Civil Rights more than three year ago, alleging that black students were being discriminated against based on race. That OCR investigation is ongoing.

Following the racial epithet incident, The Capital reported that "School administrators are investigating the incident and will take appropriate disciplinary action once the person or persons responsible for the graffiti are identified."

It should not surprise anyone that with Anne Arundel County Public Schools now closed for the summer, no one have been disciplined for this racial incident. This is becoming a pattern.

Last year, on the first day of school at Severn Middle School, racist, anti-Semitic and homophobia lyrics were posted on a county school resource website. School officials announced that an investigation was being conducted in that incident as well. On Dec. 31, it was announced no one would be charged in this racially charged incident. Another Capital headline read, "Investigation into racist blackboard post results in no charges."

Politicians and school administrators know that if you want to bury a story, you make an announcement on New Year's Eve. Chances are very few people will be paying attention.

But taxpayers, parents and students are paying attention. Parents should not have to endure incidents that inflame racial tensions or create hostile environment for students. When a student was arrested at Severna Park High School earlier this year for threatening students who wore rainbow ribbons supporting gay rights, it sent a clear message: that these threats were being taken seriously.

African-American students and parents need to believe that their children's safety merits the same response. Given what has happened around the nation involving schools and violence, all parents must be assured that their children's safety is of paramount concern, regardless of their race, gender, religion or sexual orientation.

It is my hope that over the summer months Anne Arundel County school officials develop a better system for preventing these occurrences.

The one thing that we do know is that when "investigations" are announced, no one should hold his or her breath waiting for the outcome. The outcome is predictable, which is precisely why this column was necessary.

Carl Snowden: An 'apology' doesn't go far enough

February 27, 2017

On Monday, descendants of the only Marylander to serve as chief justice of the U.S. Supreme Court plan to go to the statue of Roger B. Taney in front of the State House to issue an "apology" for the court's infamous decision in Dred Scott v. Sandford, issued on March 6, 1857.

The 7-2 decision said, in effect, that black people had no rights white people were bounded to respect. The Supreme Court 7-2 decision said Dred Scott, a slave who had been taken to free territory, could not sue in federal court to escape servitude. It was the most racist decision the Supreme Court ever handed down, affirming for white supremacists their belief that white people were superior to blacks — a lie that, 160 years later, reminds us how deeply rooted racism was in this nation by law, custom and practice.

A guest column in The Capital a few years ago by Anne Arundel County Circuit Court Judge Paul G. Goetzke defended Taney, saying in essence that he was a "man of his times" and should be judged that way. It's the same logic some apply to slaveholding Founding Fathers. We are told Thomas Jefferson, who wrote the magnificent words, "We hold these truths to be self-evident, that all men are created equal" should be given a pass on the fact he owned slaves.

Soon after the Civil War, the state commissioned the statue of Taney on the State House grounds. Thousands of tourists pass it every year, most with no idea of who Taney was or why he occupies such a prominent location.

Twenty years ago, civil rights advocates pressured the state into erecting a statue of Thurgood Marshall, the Marylander who was the first African-American justice on the Supreme Court, on Lawyers Mall. Some say this "balances" Taney's statue. I respectfully disagree.

Taney's descendants are to be joined on Monday, as a gesture of support, by William Haley, the son of Alex Haley, and other descendants of Kunta Kinte, brought to Annapolis in chains in 1767. But reconciliation, unless it is accompanied by reparations, is a hollow gesture.

How does an "apology" address slavery, the Middle Passage, the Jim Crow laws, the lynchings, the institutional racism and the dreadful Dred Scott decision, which led to so many atrocities during the more than a century of oppression, exploitation and degradation it sanctioned.

The men who wore black robes in 1857 were in sync with the men who later wore white robes and terrorized black people. These terrorists and night riders agreed with the reasoning of the Dred Scott decision.

I have no doubt of the sincerity of the well-meaning people organizing Monday's apology. But for this gesture to mean anything, it must be accompanied by action that seeks to remedy the situation.

There is ample precedent. In 1988, Congress gave reparations to Japanese-Americans whose families were interned during World War II. Congress entered into treaties with Native Americans to compensate them for land that was confiscated. In 1953, West Germany and Israel entered into the Luxembourg Agreement, resulting in reparations for Jewish victims of the Holocaust.

There has been nothing equivalent for African-Americans. In the final days of the Civil War, on Jan. 16, 1865, Union Gen. William T. Sherman, trying to go beyond Lincoln's Emancipation Proclamation in addressing the wrongs of slavery, promised formerly enslaved African-American farmers 40 acres and a mule — something that never happened.

I commend the organizers of Monday's event. But if justice means anything, it must mean more than a symbolic gesture — it must be accompanied by real reform. The organizers should seriously consider asking the state to follow their apology with action resulting in reparations. You can bet that this would put Maryland in the vanguard of real change.

I wish the organizers luck, but I think they will discover that issuing an apology, by itself, will neither change history nor make amends for America's greatest sin.

Carl Snowden: Symbols of hate draw a response from many

October 10, 2017

In our society, there are so many events it is sometimes difficult to keep up with them. In particular, we read about alleged hate crimes so often that they seem to have become "normal."

Yet we must make sure that this is not the case.

Earlier this year, we saw neo-Nazis and Ku Klux Klansmen marching in Charlottesville, Virginia, and witnessed the death of an innocent woman, Heather Heyer.

Who would have believed that white supremacists have become so emboldened that they no longer wear hoods in public but proudly display their hate for the whole world to see? Anyone who witnessed that march of hate and who knows anything about history knows that we must take all hate crimes seriously.

On May 20, newly commissioned Army 2nd Lt. Richard Collins III, who was African-American, was fatally stabbed at a bus stop on the campus of the University of Maryland, College Park. A Severna Park native, Sean Urbanski, has been charged with the crime.

Lt. Collins was days away from his graduation at Bowie State University graduate. His promising future was cut short. Mr. Urbanski's trial is scheduled for early next year in neighboring Prince George's County.

In a nine days, the so-called noose trial will start in Anne Arundel County Circuit Court, although it will involve only one of the original two defendants.

Conner Prout, 19, of Crofton, and John Havermann, also 19, of Pasadena, were charged with committing or conspiring to commit a hate crime after a May 11 incident in which a noose was hung from a light fixture outside a classroom at Crofton Middle School, whose student body is about 20 percent African-American and which has a black principal.

The arrests came after police reviewed video surveillance footage that showed two men on the school roof in the early morning hours.

Last week it was announced that Mr. Prout had accepted a plea agreement negotiated with the county branch of the NAACP, after State's Attorney Wes Adams approached the organization's leadership with the idea.

Instead of jail time, Mr. Prout was given 18 months of probation, which will include 120 hours of community service overseen by the NAACP. Writing about this arrangement in *The Sunday Capital,* the branch president, the Rev. Stephen A. Tillett, said he doubted imprisoning Mr. Prout would "result in the greater good for the community."

At Mr. Prout's sentencing, Judge J. Michael Wachs said he found it hard to believe the 19-year-old's contention that he didn't realize the noose had racist connotations.

As of this writing, the case against Mr. Havermann — who, according to an assistant state's attorney, has admitted to being the instigator of the incident — is set to go to trial on Oct. 19. This case will be closely monitored by the public.

This evening at 6 the Caucus of African-American Leaders will meet at the Wiley H. Bates Legacy Center, 1101 Smithville St. in Annapolis. The meeting is open to the public and will serve to provide an update on these and other cases that have generated controversy and concern.

Both the Anne Arundel County branch of the NAACP and the Caucus of African-American Leaders have called on citizens to be patient as these cases move forward.

Nooses and swastikas are symbols that have been used to oppress, exploit, disenfranchise and kill people. The proponents of white supremacy are discovering that there are many people in this nation who will not allow them to take us back to a dark past.

We are determined that the future will be brighter for our children and grandchildren. Despite the actions of racists and anti-Semites, we boldly say *A Luta Continua*, which in Portuguese means that the struggle for racial equality, peace and justice continues!

Carl Snowden: Issues of racism in Anne Arundel County Public Schools, Maryland government must be dealt with

May 07, 2018

Tuesday's 6 p.m. meeting of the Caucus of African-American Leaders at the Wiley H. Bates Legacy Center, 1101 Smithville St. in Annapolis, will deal with two contentious issues that have received wide coverage in the media.

On Feb. 13th, The Capital reported that a formal complaint was filed with Maryland Department of Transportation Secretary Pete K. Rahn alleging racism and bullying at the State Highway Administration.

Responding to complaints he received from his constituents on this matter, House of Delegates Speaker Michael E. Busch wrote to Secretary Rahn, in a letter dated Feb. 15, that the allegations of bullying and disparate treatment were "extremely alarming and must be investigated immediately." That was almost 90 days ago.

Tuesday the public will receive an update on this investigation, with SHA employees who have met with Speaker Busch sharing their findings.

The most contentious issue, however, is the systemic racism the Anne Arundel County branch of the NAACP and the Caucus of African-American Leaders allege continues to plague the school system.

In 2012, the NAACP filed a complaint on this with the U.S. Department of Education's Office of Civil Rights. That complaint is still being investigated.

There have been at least a dozen complaints alleging racial discrimination over the years. In the best known — on May 14, 2004, the 50th anniversary of the U.S. Supreme Court's Brown v. Board of Education ruling — local civil rights groups, clergy and black elected and appointed officials all alleged racism. A mediated settlement by the U.S. Department of Justice resulted in an agreement in 2005 between the school system and the complainants to close the achievement gap between white and minority students. But that achievement gap remains.

Recent years have seen an uptick in ugly racial incidents in county schools.

After the hanging of a noose at Crofton Middle School, one defendant was convicted of a hate crime and another was acquitted on the same charges. African-American parents said their children have been subjected to daily insults and racial epithets at Chesapeake High School. One student alleged that his teacher called him a racial slur. That teacher, who retired, never apologized.

There have been disturbing incidents at other schools, including Severn Middle School and North County, Southern, Glen Burnie and Severna Park high schools.

More often than not, the culprits in these acts haven't been apprehended by law enforcement officials. So what can be done to curtail these acts of bigotry?

We have invited former U.S. Secretary of Education John B. King Jr. to come and share his views. He will be addressing the caucus promptly at 6, but the doors will open at 5 and a complimentary dinner and beverage will be served.

We have invited the entire Anne Arundel County Board of Education and all candidates seeking office to attend this important event. School Board President Julie Hummer, schools Superintendent George Arlotto and members of his staff will be in attendance. Also in attendance will be state legislators and members of the county and Annapolis city councils. These elected officials are interested in hearing what can be done to address an issue that has caused so much divisiveness in our community.

Nelson Mandela once said, "Education is the most powerful weapon that you can use to the change the world." Malcolm X said, "Education is the passport to the future, for tomorrow belongs to those who prepare for it today."

On Tuesday Secretary King will be speaking to an audience of educators, activists, parents and students who believe that both Malcolm and Mandela are correct. They want an opportunity to have their children learn in an educational environment devoid of nooses, racial slurs and hostility.

They do not think that is too much to ask, and neither do I.

A Luta Continua, which in Portuguese means that the struggle continues for justice, equality and peace.

Carl Snowden: State needs to investigate BWI fire department and SHA complaints

July 09, 2018

Anne Arundel County has two major things named after the late Associate Justice Thurgood Marshall. In Annapolis, there is the Thurgood Marshall Statue, which is located prominently at Lawyer's Mall near the State House. The BWI Thurgood Marshall Airport also carries the name of Justice Marshall.

Last month, Maryland Gov. Larry Hogan and the Board of Public Works unanimously approved a settlement involving the black deputy chief of the BWI fire department. Deputy Chief Gregory Lawrence had sued the State of Maryland for racial discrimination three times and has won all three cases. These lawsuits occurred over a seven-year period.

When he first applied for employment seven years ago, he was denied. He sued and won. He became the first African-American deputy fire chief. He later was fired by the fire department. He sued them again.

In that case, administrative law Judge Nancy E. Paige wrote in her 54-page decision that "I conclude that the employee would not have been terminated if he were not African-American." Also, she found that a "racially inhospitable environment" existed at the BWI Thurgood Marshall Airport's fire department.

The State of Maryland appealed her decision and lost. Lawrence was represented by the late renowned Annapolis civil rights attorney Alan H. Legum. The court ordered that Mr. Lawrence return to work. Legum told The Sun at the time that the judge's order should be a "wake-up" call for state officials.

"They've been found by a neutral judge to have racially discriminated against Chief Lawrence, if that doesn't get your attention, I don't know what will," Legum said.

In the current case, settled last month, Lawrence applied to become chief of the BWI Fire Department. Despite serving as acting chief, he was denied the job.

He retained the services of attorney Shane Nikolao, the former law partner of Legum. The case was settled in federal District Court. One would think that someone would be asking what is going on? They are not.

The airport, which is under Maryland Department of Transporation, its secretary, Peter K. Ryan, was notified earlier this year by Speaker Michael Busch of alleged bullying and discrimination in the State Highway Administration, which is also under Secretary Ryan.

State Highway Administration employees have complained about racial discrimination, bullying, sexual harassment and more. Sidney Proctor and Anthony Johnson have met with Speaker Busch, who has written to Secretary Ryan and as of this writing, there has been no resolution of their concerns.

It seems to me that Deputy Lawrence's cases indicate that there is a need to have an independent review of the BWI Fire Department and the State Highway Administration.

Taxpayers shouldn't be put on the financial hook for alleged racial discrimination.

On another note, I want to add my condolences to the families and victims of the mass murder that took place at The Capital newspaper last month. The late Gerald Fischman edited my column for years. He was a magnificent human being. Wendi Winters and I often saw each other at the gym. We would talk about politics and world events. Rob Hiaasen often participated in the quarterly meetings that took place at The Capital with members of the community.

Tonight we will honor them, Rebecca Smith and John McNamara at the Caucus of African-American Leaders meeting, which will begin with a 5 p.m. reception at the Wiley H. Bates Legacy Center, 1101 Smithville Street, Annapolis. There will be a complimentary dinner served.

Our meetings are open to the public and we have invited Rick Hutzell, editor of The Capital to address our membership. Dr. Martin Luther King, Jr. once said, "darkness cannot drive out darkness; only light can do that. Hate cannot drive out hate; only love can do that."

Tuesday, we want to let the employees of The Capital know that they are not the "enemy of the people," but, rather, they serve an important role bringing "light" to things that have been in the dark for far too long. This evening, we honor the memory of those who lost their lives through a senseless act of violence.

Carl Snowden: Meeting exposed racial issues

July 23, 2018

Last week, at a jam-packed Anne Arundel County Council meeting, citizens in attendance and those watching on live television saw their elected government close up and in color.

The seven-member County Council has no women on it and one lone African-American, Councilman Pete Smith.

Citizens who came to the meeting to express their views on a resolution denouncing hate acts and crimes following the death of U.S. Army 2nd Lt. Richard Wilbur Collins III found themselves being cut off numerous times by County Council Chairman John Grasso.

Mr. Grasso took exception to the fact that many of the speakers wanted to address the alleged hate-group ties of Councilman Michael Peroutka. Those people were told by Mr. Grasso that they would not be allowed to speak about any hate groups that Mr. Peroutka may have been associated with.

Time and time again, the chairman bellowed and screamed that he would not permit speakers to express their views on the subject of Mr. Peroutka's alleged ties.

Mr. Grasso was reminded that there is something called the First Amendment. He was reminded by Amy Cruice, of the American Civil Liberties Union of Maryland, that citizens had a right to petition their government and to express their views.

This is what makes the American government different from other governments around the world. You can actually criticize your representatives.

The public servants on the County Council, when they were elected, knew that citizens would sometimes disagree with them. But despite this fundamental right, the chairman continued to cut off debate.

Councilman Smith, who introduced the resolution against hatred and bias, after giving a passionate speech about a racial experience he had as a teenager, talked about how, more than 25 years later, he is still traumatized by that experience.

When Councilman Smith concluded, Chairman Grasso thanked Councilman Smith and called him a "boy." When it was pointed out by this writer that it was inappropriate to refer to a grown black man as a "boy," the chairman continued, without offering an apology to Mr. Smith or the audience, which also was offended by his remarks.

In fact, when a woman told Mr. Grasso she thought that he owed not only Mr. Smith but her congressman, U.S. Rep. Anthony Brown, an apology for calling him an "idiot" in a Facebook posting, Mr. Grasso again refused to apologize.

Rep. Brown, who is African-American, is a former lieutenant governor, a delegate and a graduate of Harvard University and Harvard Law School. He may be many things, but an "idiot" he is not.

Last week's County Council meeting gave attendees and television viewers a firsthand look at their government in action.

The anti-hate resolution was eventually amended to denounce white supremacists and unanimously passed the County Council.

Speaker after speaker said that the resolution was just a first step. The reality is that it really unveiled some serious racial undertones in Anne Arundel County.

It may seem to some to be OK to call black elected officials "boy" and "idiot," but many of us in attendance realized that we have a lot of work to do as we prepare for the 2018 election.

The Caucus of African-American Leaders meets on the second Tuesday of each month at the Wiley H. Bates Legacy Center, 1101 Smithville St. in Annapolis. This meeting is open to the public as we continue to keep Dr. King's legacy alive.

We invite Mr. Grasso and Mr. Peroutka to attend. What they will discover is a group of people who understand that civility isn't name-calling or shouting down your opponents, but being willing to listen.

We understand that the struggle for racial equality and peace continues in Anne Arundel County, which is precisely why I always end this column with *A Luta Continua*, which in Portuguese means that the struggle continues!

Carl Snowden: Lawsuit shines a light on Annapolis public housing

June 10, 2019

When The Capital reported on their front page on July 25, 1984, that "HUD finds bias in Annapolis's housing plans" it generated stories across the region.

It was the first time in the history of the City of Annapolis that the federal government had found that the city government had knowingly discriminated against African-Americans based on their race and color in their housing policies.

The then-Mayor Richard L. Hillman acknowledged the problem. The report was both damming and alarming. Yet, nothing happened. It became just another story about racism and its corrosive impact on a community of color.

Then, last month, 35 years later, a lawsuit brought by Annapolis attorney Joseph Donahue and the Maryland Legal Aid Bureau representing residents living in public housing alleged that they are the victims of a continuing and systemic racism. In the lawsuit filed in federal court in Baltimore, the 111-page lawsuit in vivid details lay out a painful history of racism.

The lawsuit says: "The historical record is clear: Annapolis was integral in the perpetuation of the African slave trade, which resulted in the subjugation of newly imported Africans to white slaveholders."

The lawsuit gives readers a history that they will not find in the curriculum in Anne Arundel County Public Schools and they will be hard pressed to find it at Anne Arundel Community College. What this lawsuit does is hold up a mirror and what you see is frightening.

The authors of this enlightening lawsuit says: "As the Civil Rights movement was taking hold across the nation, the City of Annapolis, in cooperation with HACA, moved its African-American residents away from the City Center. These residents were provided public housing units, and many, then stripped of their livelihood, were congregated into dense developments scattered miles from employment opportunities and without a viable transportation system. Given no alternative, the once vibrant community was decimated, and its population crammed into public housing against their will. The African American residents of Annapolis have never recovered from the 1960s urban renewal policies of the City of Annapolis."

The lawsuit brings a bright light to problems that existed in the shadows before either Mayor Gavin Buckley or the soon to be retiring CEO of the Housing Authority for the City of Annapolis Beverly Wilbourne ever came on the scene. They inherited a history that they did not create. Yet, they must provide a blueprint for a brighter future.

At 6 p.m. on Tuesday at the Wiley H. Bates Legacy Center, 1101 Smithville Street, Annapolis, Maryland, a forum will be held on The Future of Public Housing.

What does Buckley and County Executive Steuart Pittman propose to do about shrinking federal dollars and a growing aging housing stock? How do people living in public housing transition out? What do they do about allege police brutality and crime?

These and other provocative questions will be addressed at the forum on public housing. Complimentary parking, food and beverages will be provided. A social hour begins at 5 pm followed by the meeting at 6 p.m.

Invited to attend the forum are state Sen. Sarah Elfreth, Del. Alice Cain, Del. Shaneka Henson, Del. Mike Rogers, Councilwoman Lisa Brannigan Rodvien, the entire County and City Councils. Why? Because ultimately with the residents of public housing they must decide both its future and fate.

Carl Snowden: Pittman's work on memorial, racist graffiti show collaboration with community

July 22, 2019

The Caucus of African-American Leaders is a consortium of organizations, elected officials and civil rights activists that meets monthly to discuss issues with elected officials, including Mayor Gavin Buckley and County Executive Steuart Pittman. These meetings, for the most part, have been very productive.

On Wednesday we will meet with County Executive Pittman and among the issues, we will be discussing is the county executive's commitment to building the memorial to the journalists and staff, who were murdered last year at The Capital newspaper headquarters.

This memorial, which will be located downtown on city-owned land and funded by the county and private donors is a testament to what government working in collaboration with its citizens can do.

Another example of that collaboration was Pittman's strong condemnation of the racist graffiti that was placed at the Mayo skate park. The graffiti contained a racial slur and an image of a man being lynched.

The graffiti was first reported to the Anne Arundel County police on June 26. It received wide coverage when WTTG-TV reported on it. It has since been sprayed over.

Pittman's condemnation was welcomed by his constituents who were assured that white supremacists and bigots had no ally in the Office of the County Executive.

How many times have we seen racist remarks, tweets, and insults go unchallenged by elected officials? The answer is too many times.

Quite frankly, it was a welcome relief to have an elected official use the power of his office in such a manner that made clear he will not tolerate racism.

The powerful comments of Police Chief Timothy Altomare, in which he opined, "Racism has no home here in Anne Arundel County. Your police department condemns hateful ideology with every ounce of our being and we will investigate and prosecute such cases to the fullest extent of the law."

Today more than ever, we need leaders who are willing to roll up their sleeves and do the heavy lifting. Our county, like our nation is at a crossroad. We can decide to work together to solve problems or we can remain a divided nation.

Locally, some of our elected officials have decided to collaborate and work to ensure that all citizens voices are heard.

It is refreshing to have leaders who are more interested in what kind of society we will leave for our children and grandchildren to inherit, than their next election.

I end this column with this African proverb. "If you want to go fast, go alone. If you want to go far, go together."

A Luta Continua, which means in Portuguese that the struggle continues to create a society where racism will not have a home.

Carl Snowden: To understand where we are, watch people

September 23, 2019

I am fond of saying that while some people watch clocks to tell what time it is, I watch people and I know what time it is.

You can learn a lot just by paying attention and listening. Over the years, thanks to the late Morris H. Blum, the founder of WANN radio, I was given an opportunity to meet a lot of people, who later would provide me with invaluable insight on so many issues.

As a moderator for a WANN's public affairs program, I was able to interview so many people including James Baldwin, Rosa Parks, Dick Gregory, Jack Anderson, Stokley Carmichael, Ralph Nadler, the Rev. Jesse Jackson, Alex Haley, Julian Bond, Mayor Maynard Jackson, Eldridge Cleaver, U.S. Rep. Barbara Jordan, and the late U.S. Rep. Parren J. Mitchell to name just a few.

Years later, I was hired by WJZ-TV in Baltimore as a commentator and a panelist. I met Oprah Winfrey, who I later got to speak at Meade Village, a public housing community in Severn. Each of these people gave me a unique perspective on the struggle for equality and peace.

One of my best friends was the late prominent Annapolis civil rights attorney Alan Legum. We would meet for a leisurely lunch and discuss books that we had read. He would often recommend some new book and I would read it and we would spend hours just talking.

There are two experiences that I would like to share with readers, both, has to do with paying attention and listening. While a moderator on WANN, I invited a leader of the Ku Klux Klan to be interviewed. He came to the radio station with a bodyguard and all of the ignorance that is associated with his organization. He talked disparagingly about Jews, African-Americans, Catholics and a host of other perceived "undesirables."

His racism was so evident that it didn't take long to debunk his nonsense. As I watched and listened, I saw a man, who was frightened and whose world was changing rapidly and he couldn't do a thing about it.

The other interview that stands out is the interview I did with the late Stokley Carmichael who later changed his name to Kwame Ture. Stokley was the exact opposite of the leader of the Klan, he was articulate, passionate and knowledgeable.

What I didn't know until much later, the FBI had recorded and transcribed the entire interview that I did with Carmichael. I only discovered this after successfully suing the FBI under the Freedom of Information and getting access to my FBI file. I actually donated the complete file to the American Civil Liberties Union of Maryland and they have placed the entire file on their website so that anyone who wants to see it can. You can call the ACLU at 410-889-8550 to obtain the location.

I have been active for more than a half-century. I have seen many things and have I have met many people - Some famous, and some nondescript. What I have learned is that if you pay attention and listen you can learn a great deal about what time it is.

JUSTICE & INJUSTICE

Alderman Samuel Gilmer; Annapolis Mayor Dean Johnson;
U.S. Congressman Elijah Cummings; Senator Barbara Mikulski;
Governor Parris Glendening; and Carl O. Snowden.

The columns that were written for this chapter were all designed to raise hell and consciousness at the same time. I have always been incensed by injustice. Dr. Martin Luther King, Jr.'s assertion "that injustice anywhere is a threat to justice everywhere" is for me a fact of life.

The injustice perpetrated by law enforcement and the government has always been a burden that too many people of color have experienced. Whether it is a police shooting innocent citizens or a president abusing his power, the result is always the same.

People have lost faith in their institutions. There can be no peace until there is justice. It has become "normal" to read about and to see on television wrongful police shootings and corruption. People do not believe the system is working for them. Whether it is the criminal justice system or the government, people have lost confidence in these institutions.

Those who followed closely the Freddie Gray disturbances in Baltimore knew that when politicians and preachers urged rioting youth to allow the city to return to "normal", they were following a long tradition.

That tradition has included an unjust murder, followed by days of rioting and looting. An increase of police and National Guardsmen and a show of force and then a return to "normalcy" or in the words of Malcolm X, "don't stop suffering, just suffer peacefully."

The current ongoing saga of President Donald Trump is one of the issues I take on in this chapter. I know that people believe that the end has already been predetermined. However, events have a way of intervening in the best-laid plans of man. As you read this chapter, remember that "injustice anywhere is a threat to justice everywhere".

Carl Snowden: Facts don't need to be 'cherry-picked'

May 24, 2016

In politics, there are the fraternal twins: ignorance and arrogance. Ignorance tends to ignore history and arrogance refuses to learn its lessons.

Last week, I attended an Annapolis City Council Public Safety Committee meeting to share information I had acquired. After waiting patiently for more than an hour, I brought to the committee's attention my belief that an African-American police officer, Jason Thomas, received disparate treatment.

I pointed out that Thomas, who recently appeared before the city's Public Safety Retirement Board, was never informed that a member of that tribunal, Sgt. Jessica Kirchner, admitted filing a false police report in a sworn deposition in an unrelated federal court trial. I said I believed this should have been disclosed by the Office of the City Attorney, but was not. I pointed out that this information was in a sworn deposition in a federal court case the city had recently won.

In addition, they were made aware of newspaper articles reported that Sgt. Christopher Kintop, a subject of a recently filed federal civil rights lawsuit, had also been found liable in a local District Court case, in which the city was required to pay damages to a citizen. I raised the possibility that cases Kintop may be involved in may be dismissed because of this court's finding, as has happened in similar instances.

City Attorney Michael G. Leahy, Assistant City Attorney Gary M. Elson and police Chief Michael Pristoop all joined in denouncing my "characterization" of these facts. Elson took great pains to attack The Capital for the alleged great harm it did to Kintop.

Alderman Ross Arnett, present at the hearing but not a member of the panel, accused me of "cherry-picking" the facts and giving a divisive presentation. I waited to hear which "facts" I had gotten wrong.

I've served three terms on the City Council and understand the constant posturing of politicians. I was not the least bit offended by the vigorous defense city officials put forward. My purpose, as a taxpayer and citizen, was to voice my opinion. Robust discussion is essential to democracy and elected officials have a responsibility to listen to the public and remember that they are public servants.

Attacking the media and the messenger is a convenient tactic to distract from the issue at hand. The documents I provided members of the City Council confirmed that these officers received adverse decisions that arose from various court proceedings. The facts were not in dispute.

Immediately after the meeting adjourned, I was approached by Leahy, the city attorney, whom I respect. We had a very civil conversation. I shared my perspective and he shared his. Neither of us hold elected positions, so there was no reason to grandstand and make outrageous allegations about cherry-picking. We agreed to disagree.

I believe that Thomas was entitled to know a person who had judged his truthfulness had herself filed a false police report. I think most people believe transparency is required in order that justice is served.

I knew before making my comments that in a city where the fraternal twins, ignorance and arrogance, reign, some would be upset.

But years ago, I discovered two truisms.

First, whenever you speak truth to power, you need not fear what the outcome will be. Second, in a city noted for its sailing and boating, in order to make progress you have to make waves.

Politicians come and go — it is a statesman who makes the difference in this world. I leave it to the readers to decide whether they believe that Thomas had a right to know that one of his panel members had false filed a police report.

But when I come to the naughty fraternal twins of ignorance and arrogance, my response to will always be the same: *A Luta Continua*, which in Portuguese means the struggle continues for truth, justice and freedom of speech.

Carl Snowden: Pittman's transition team finds bullying, retaliation in Central Services

May 28, 2019

Whenever a new administration is elected to the office, a group of volunteers is appointed to a transition team. In the case of Anne Arundel County Executive Steuart Pittman, he appointed more than 200 volunteers to serve on various committees, when he was elected last year.

The transition team was chaired by former County Executive Janet Owens and former Councilman Chris Trumbauer. Some of the members serving on the transition team included former councilmen Daryl Jones and Jerry Walker.

Having served on the transition teams in the past, it is not unusual for the recommendations of a transition team to wind up on a bookshelf to later be dusted off by a new administration.

However, in the case of the Steuart Pittman Transition Team subcommittee report which was entitled "Responsive Government Transition Committee Central Services Subcommittee Report," I found something that was very disconcerting and alarming. It was something that required his immediate attention.

A subcommittee whose members were: Amy Lanham, Kim Pruim, William Schull and Lonnie Lancione wrote the following:

"The subcommittee focused mainly on processes and tried to refrain from matters of personnel, however, employees within the department and who deal directly with the departments swarmed to express unsolicited concerns regarding what they describe as a punitive environment with little or no support and fear of retaliation and bullying at any questioning of current or past practices."

The subcommittee on Central Services further stated: "Complaints referred to the Office of Personnel were not kept confidential leaving employees no resource but to seek other employment."

These and other statements included the following statements:

"Several that have separated from employment taking years of experience with them, those individuals describe the environment as a dictatorship often leaving employees in tears."

I could not believe what I was reading. Bullying, dictatorship, retaliation, and employees violating personnel issues that are supposed to be confidential. These allegations all exist in a public document on the county government's webpage.

The Caucus of African-American Leaders wrote last week to Pittman noting that his new Personnel Director, Sherri Dickerson, Alanna W. Dennis, Equal Employment Opportunity director, and Janice Hayes Williams, director of minority engagement and advancement, should be dispatched immediately to address these serious concerns.

Dee Goodwyn a retired human resources vice-president of a major corporation who is a member of the caucus said: "Since managers are on the front lines with the employees they need to be reminded of the backlash they could face showing their biases when retaliating against employees. Perhaps some type of management diversity training is necessary."

She further said: "Also it may help keep the Administration from potential and/or unnecessary civil rights violations and lawsuits."

Pittman directed Dennis to begin an inquiry. Government employees should not be subject to a hostile work environment. Nor should their pleas go unanswered.

I applaud the subcommittee on Central Services for bringing to the public attention these employees concerns.

Pittman has pledged to make Anne Arundel County "the best place."

Let's hope he starts by making Anne Arundel County government the best place to work. A workplace that is free of bullying, retaliation, dictatorship, and where confidentiality is respected and employees are protected.

Carl Snowden: Black history belongs in schools, homes

June 10, 2019

We are in the ninth day of "Black History Month" — though, in reality, black history is American history. February has been set aside by the federal government to encourage Americans to learn more about the contributions African-Americans have made to the nation. It also serves as a barometer of how far we have come as a nation. Many Americans are woefully ignorant about history in general, and when it comes to African-American history it is even worse.

Many are surprised to learn that the first black elected official in Maryland was Alderman William H. Butler, elected to the Annapolis City Council in 1873, just eight years after the Civil War.

They are equally shocked to learn that lynchings occurred in Anne Arundel County. In 1921, Henry Davis was lynched near the campus of St. John's College for allegedly assaulting a white woman in Crownsville. More than 50 whites overpowered guards at the old jail, on the site of today's Arundel Center. Mr. Davis was shot over 100 times. Photographs were taken of his mutilated body and sold as postcards. A grand jury was convened, but no one was ever convicted.

Most also don't know the history of the struggle for voting rights. The NAACP was founded in 1909, one year after the General Assembly enacted a "grandfather" law: If your grandfather had the right to vote, so did you. This disenfranchised thousands of African-Americans. Because of this law, blacks had no representation from 1906 until 1915 on the Annapolis City Council.

In 1915, the Republican Party and a group of Annapolis blacks sued to get the law overturned. The U.S. Supreme Court sided with them. Yes, there was a time African-Americans voted Republican, because the GOP was considered the party of Abraham Lincoln. That changed nationally when blacks overwhelmingly voted for President John F. Kennedy in 1960.

From 1873 until 1981, every black elected to the Annapolis City Council was a Republican. Alderman Samuel Gilmer was the first black Democrat on the council; Sarah Carter was the first African-American woman elected to the Anne Arundel County Council. Only three blacks have ever been elected to the council — the other two are Daryl Jones and current Councilman Pete Smith.

Only one black — Aris T. Allen Sr., elected as a delegate and later appointed as a state senator – has represented Anne Arundel County in the General Assembly. Most of the thousands of motorists who drive down Aris T. Allen Boulevard are oblivious to who he was.

Of the two Marylanders who have served on the U.S. Supreme Court, one was Chief Justice Roger C. Taney — whose infamous Dred Scott decision that said, in essence, blacks had no rights whites were bound to respect — and the other was Associate Justice Thurgood Marshall, who successfully argued the case for Walter Mills, who fought for and won equal pay for white and black teachers in this county.

Many of these important facts aren't reflected in the county's public school curriculum. Our children — white, black, brown, red and yellow — need to know their history.

The Caucus of African-American Leaders meets on the second Tuesday of each month at the Wiley H. Bates Legacy Center, 1101 Smithville St. in Annapolis. This meeting is open to the public as we continue to keep Dr. King's legacy alive. Parents and activists will have an opportunity to talk about this and other matters.

While I am strong proponent of holding our public schools accountable and making sure that they are inclusive, I have become convinced that if our children are truly to learn their history, then it needs to start at home. Just as we have Sunday schools to teach religion, we need Saturday Schools to preserve our history.

Some things never change, and that is the value of knowing your history. It is also why, I always end this column with the Portuguese slogan *A Luta Continua*, which means "the struggle continues."

Carl Snowden: Critics of President Trump like Lewis Bracy should be patient — change will come

June 25, 2019

Retired National Security Agency police officer Lewis Bracy, a resident of Hanover, and former CIA Director John Brennan share one thing in common: they believe that President Donald Trump is a threat to the nation.

Ironically, they are not the only ones from the intelligence community that believes it. So does James Clapper, the former NSA director and director of national intelligence, ex CIA director Michael Hayden, former FBI director James Comey, who President Trump fired and many others.

It is so unusual to see people who generally operate in the shadows so public. Do you remember when "NSA" employees said that it stood for no such agency?

Bracy's contempt for President Trump is so great, he has protested in front of the White House and the Justice Department. His placard leaves no doubt about his animus toward the president.

He has written letters to both U.S. Rep. Steny Hoyer and Dutch Ruppersberger demanding that they impeach the president.

He has called on U.S. Senators Ben Cardin and Chris Van Hollen to join him in calling for the impeachment of the president.

He strongly believes that the president has not only violated the law but has colluded with foreign nations to increase his own personal wealth.

There is probably no president in modern history that has riled the intelligence community like Trump.

Certainly, no one can remember the last time more than 700 federal prosecutors both Republicans and Democrats signed onto an open letter against a president.

The open letter that said that if President Trump was not a sitting president, he would have been charged with obstruction of justice based off the evidence laid out in special counsel Robert Mueller's report to the Congress.

Mr. Bracy is adamant that Congress is not exercising its responsibilities under the U.S. Constitution. He is incensed that President Trump has not been impeached by the Democratically controlled House of Representatives.

Now, here is some advice that I have for both Bracy and those who share his views. Be patient. Sometimes it appears that nothing will stick to Trump. His countless misstatements, tweets of insults or gaffes.

His denigration of the late Sen. John McCain, all seem to think they have had no impact on the president's political fortunes. I disagree.

Last year's mid-term elections I believe is a dress rehearsal for what is coming. Sometimes people do not appreciate history. Voters have a way of righting a situation.

Remember what happened following the resignation of President Richard Nixon in 1974? Voters took the nation in an entirely new direction.

I am convinced that our democracy while being challenged will survive. I believe that people are paying attention to what members of the intelligence community have been saying.

What I further believe is that Bracy, Clapper, and Brennan are patriots. They love their nation.

When we celebrate the Fourth of July, it is the people that have often been in the shadows that make it possible for us to enjoy the sunlight of democracy that we have.

However, for these critics of the president, I would simply remind them of what another great patriot named Martin Luther King, Jr. said, "The greatest march that an American can participate in, is the march to the ballot box."

Also, he reminded us that the "arc of the universe is long, but it bends toward justice". Patience is not only a virtue, but it is also a necessity in these trying times.

A Luta Continua, which means in Portuguese that the struggle continues for a society where no one is above the law.

EDUCATION

Jacqueline Allsup; Congressman John Lewis; Carl O. Snowden; Police Chief
Joseph Johnson; Mayor Josh Cohen; Daryl Jones, Esq.; and Marc Apter.

The late great satirist Dick Gregory often made the astute observation that there is a difference between education and indoctrination. Education should be a process which allows individuals to learn how to think for themselves – a life-long journey that has an insatiable appetite for learning.

The life story of Malcolm X is a case in point. One of the many traits that impressed me about Malcolm X was his willingness to not allow dogma to interfere with his education. This is underscored in the reading of *The Autobiography of Malcolm X*. I learned what the impact of education can have on an individual and I was mesmerized by his life story.

I admired his willingness to transform his prison cell into a library. His sheer desire to learn became a lifelong obsession with him. When I have traveled to many parts of Africa, there too

I have seen and met people who, like Malcolm, were willing to make great sacrifices in order to learn.

In America, we take education for granted. When visiting Ghana I was impressed with the young people who I met who wanted an opportunity to learn. They represented a teacher's greatest dream – willing students who placed a great value on knowledge.

Many years ago, there was a great controversy involving Oprah Winfrey's decision to open a school in South Africa rather than on the Southside of Chicago. In the end, Oprah decided on South Africa. Her decision was based on the idea that the children of South Africa had placed a greater premium on education than the students on the Southside. Both time and history will determine whether she was right.

On the other hand, Indoctrination is a process that seeks to tell people how and what to think. In today's political climate, indoctrination is in full throttle as people with dogmatic views attempt to inflame rather than inform.

I believe it is important to learn how to be skeptical. President Ronald Reagan once said "trust but verify". Malcolm X and Dick Gregory had come to the same conclusion. Whether its religion or politics, don't allow some fanaticism become your compass. Always be a searcher for truth.

One of my great hopes is that black churches in America will create Saturday Schools just as they created Sunday Schools. These Saturday Schools would be dedicated to supplementing the knowledge that their children will never receive in public schools in America.

These secular schools will focus on providing children with the knowledge of their culture and their history. It will instill in them pride and confidence. They will learn in Saturday Schools what it means to be black in America and the sacrifices that their ancestors have made.

Their teachers will be a modern-day Marva Collins who see in them their great potential. The columns that I have written on this subject was with that in mind.

Carl Snowden: Education is the key to achievement

April 26, 2016

When I was growing up in a segregated America, my elders had sage advice for me and my peers. They would often say, "Get a good education. It is the one thing that they can not take away from you." That advice was quickly followed by, "You must be twice as smart to get half as far."

When I attended the segregated Carver Elementary School in Anne Arundel County, my teachers prepared me for a world in which excellence and success were synonymous.

These African-American teachers knew what was lying ahead of me. They, like my elders, wanted to make sure that I had the tools that I would need to negotiate and navigate life's journey in a nation that often saw the world in black and white. Fifty years later that prudent advice continues.

Last week, while attending a forum sponsored by the Caucus of African American Leaders and the local NAACP at St. John's United Methodist Church in the Pumphrey community regarding racially charged incidents at North County High School, I heard African-American Advanced Placement students articulate their concerns about systemic racism. They were poised and confident.

They eloquently described, in vivid and graphic details, their concerns, ranging from disparate treatment in discipline to adults not listening. Yet what impressed me most about these young students was their zest and passion. In them I saw future lawyers, entrepreneurs, professors, public servants and leaders.

What my elders instilled in me — "Get a good education" — these young people intuitively knew: that their success in life was going to be determined by getting a good education. Education is the great equalizer in life.

When I was in the 10th grade, I was required to read "The Autobiography of Malcolm X." Malcolm, an international figure who had traveled around the world, wrote these words: "My greatest lack has been, I believe, that I don't have the kind of academic education I wish I had been able to get — to have been a lawyer, perhaps. I do believe that I might have made a good lawyer." Malcolm X was assassinated in 1965.

Few would debate that Malcolm X would have been a great lawyer. His debating skills were second to none. He was a gifted orator. The message of his autobiography and his emphasis on education was not missed by the young people who attended this forum.

The world will never know what the scientist George Washington Carver might have produced if he had not been shackled by racism. I often think of what the world would have been like if we had not the voice and poetry of Maya Angelou. Can you imagine a world without the music and talent of Michael Jackson or Mahalia Jackson?

At the forum, at the church, these young gifted people were just asking for an opportunity to be allowed to live up to their full God-given potential. Racism sometimes blinds people. They do not see the possibilities.

Who would have thought in 1963 a black baby birthed by a Kansan and fathered by a man from Kenya would one day be the president of the United States of America?

As I watched these young people speak, I saw in them a future scientist who would discover the cure for cancer and AIDS. I saw in these young students ambitions and dreams, audacity and tenacity.

Long after the events at North County High School becomes a distant memory, these young people will remember the advice that their elders handed down to them, which is not unlike the advice that their parents had received: Despite the obstacles and barriers that you will face, live out your dreams a world is waiting for your gifts.

While there are others who may not understand your plight, remember the sage advised of our elders who said, "get a good education" and "be twice as smart" because these were the tools that made it possible for your elders to survive, so that you could thrive.

Carl Snowden: Advocacy for schools remains vital

May 10, 2016

On the first day of schools in Anne Arundel County, someone placed racist, anti-Semitic and homophobic messages on a blackboard school resource website at Severn River Middle School.

An investigation was launched to determine the culprit or culprits. Several months later, on the eve of the new year, State's Attorney Wes Adams, police and school officials announced that no one would be charged and the case was closed.

A few weeks ago, a North County High School student wrote an essay that many believed was racist and divisive. It was intended to be satire. The essay advocated African-Americans being eliminated through a nuclear device.

A few days after the issue became public, someone wrote a disparaging racial epithet on a bathroom wall at North County High School. School officials announced that an investigation was being launched. Sound familiar?

It has been said that those who do not learn the lessons of history are doomed to repeat it. Unfortunately, it appears history is repeating itself in our county.

I remember the eloquence of Delores Hunt, who served on the Anne Arundel County Board of Education over four decades ago. She was a strong supporter of the actions of Martha E. Wood, who died in 2000. Few reading this column even know who Wood was, but her impact on education in the county continues to be felt 45 years after she brought a civil rights complaint in 1971.

A former resident of College Creek Terrace, a public housing community in Annapolis, Mrs. Wood believed strongly in the power of education. She created the Parents Association, primarily made up of low-income residents in public housing.

The group's mission was to make sure that the children and grandchildren of its members received a quality education. They would seek resources so that children who needed tutoring or school supplies received them. They held bake sales, sold fish dinners and raised money so their children would have the tools they needed.

In 1973, Mrs. Wood filed a formal federal complaint against the county public schools alleging that black children received disparate treatment in discipline based on their race.

Sound familiar?

The complaint was filed with the Department of Heath, Education and Welfare, one of whose components became today's Department of Education.

At the time the complaint was filed, the superintendent of schools, Edward J. Anderson, said Mrs. Wood's allegations were without merit. Dr. Anderson was supported by local elected officials and most school board members. They decried her attempt at suggesting they treated children differently based on their race.

Dr. Hunt, the lone African-American board member, dissenting, making it clear that not only black children but black parents were being subject to disparate treatment.

After a four-year investigation, the federal government sided with Mrs. Wood and ordered the school system to develop a nondiscriminatory student code of conduct.

A school board-appointed committee headed by the late Rev. Robert M. Powell of St. Phillip's Church, the "Powell Commission," developed what is now known as the Student Code of Conduct. Every student is required to receive this document because of Mrs. Wood's activism.

The Caucus of African-American Leaders meets on the second Tuesday of each month at the Wiley H. Bates Legacy Center, 1101 Smithville St. in Annapolis. This meeting is open to the public as we continue to keep Dr. King's legacy alive. Stacy Korbelak, president of the school board, and former school board member Amalie Brandenburg, now the county's education officer, are scheduled to attend.

Also at this evening's meeting will be the spirit of Martha Wood, who will take note that 45 years later people are still advocating that children receive a quality education regardless of their race.

Yes, history has a way of repeating itself.

A Luta Continua, which means in Portuguese that the struggle continues.

Carl Snowden: Those who work for education advance the cause for which Medgar Evers gave up his life

June 11, 2018

Tuesday is the 55th anniversary of the assassination of Medgar Evers, the 37-year-old Mississippi field director for the NAACP.

Evers wanted his children to get the quality education he believed all children deserved. He marched, protested, organized and mobilized, energizing his community. Evers believed that if people could be registered to vote, regardless of their race, and their children had an opportunity to get a first-class education, the quality of their lives could be changed forever.

On a summer evening after he had returned from a meeting and was getting out of his car, he was shot in the back, in front of his wife and children. This cowardly act was condemned by President John F. Kennedy, Attorney General Robert F. Kennedy, Malcolm X and the Rev. Martin Luther King Jr. All decried the fact that a black man could be killed in America merely because he wanted his children to have the opportunity to receive a first-class education and the right to vote.

President Kennedy wrote Evers' widow: "Although comforting thoughts are difficult at a time like this, surely there can be some solace in the realization of the justice of the cause for which your husband gave his life. Achievements of the goals he did so much to promote will enable his children and the generations to follow to share fully and equally in the benefits and advantages that our nation has to offer."

In fewer than six months, President Kennedy, too, would become a victim of an assassin's bullet — as would happen a few years later to his brother Robert F. Kennedy, as well as the Rev. King and Malcolm X. All gave their lives so that all children in the generations that followed could have an equal share of this nation's benefits and advantages.

There is an airport named in Evers' honor in Jackson, Mississippi. There is a street named for him in Annapolis — but far too many of those living on that street are unaware of his sacrifice. The curriculum in the Anne Arundel County Public Schools doesn't explain why he was willing to die for a cause greater than himself.

Evers served in the Army in World War II, fought in the Battle of Normandy and reached the rank of sergeant. He came home to find that equal access to what all Americans want — the opportunity for a better life — was not available to him and his children.

On Tuesday, the Caucus of African-American Leaders is holding the only candidates' forum that will focus exclusively on education and equity issues. All of the candidates running for the Board of Education have been invited; many have agreed to attend.

This meeting is open to the public and seating is on a first-come, first-served basis. Kudos to Monica Lindsey and the subcommittee for helping to organize this important forum.

The confirmed moderators are Charlestine R. Fairley, a retired dean of Sojourner-Douglass College; educator Thornell Jones, a retired physicist; and Vincent O. Leggett, a former school board president. The meeting will also honor Torrington Ford, a 15-year-old who graduated from

Anne Arundel Community College and will continue his education at Ohio State University, with the Malcolm X Award for excellence in education.

The racist who shot Medgar Evers thought that he would end the movement for social justice. But as Evers once said, "You can kill a man but you can't kill an idea."

Little did the white supremacists know that the legacy of Medgar Evers would be manifested 55 years later in a voting rights campaign that he gave his life for.

A Luta Continua, which means in Portuguese that the struggle continues.

GUNS & VIOLENCE

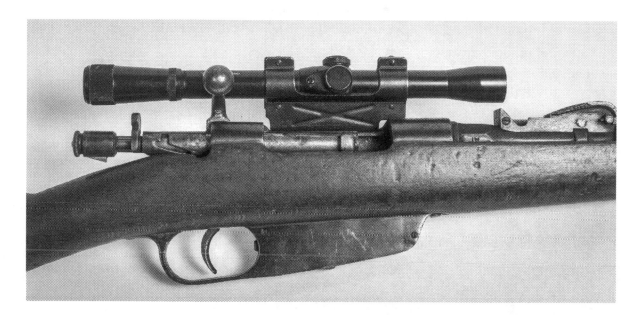

Guns and violence have played a pivotal role in the lives of American citizens. Sometimes they have resulted in the violent assassinations of political and religious leaders ranging from President John F. Kenncdy to Malcolm X. Malcolm's observation that "bullets" and not "ballots" have often changed the course of history.

Can anyone doubt that? What kind of America would we be living in had Dr. Martin Luther King, Jr. and Senator Robert F. Kennedy not been murdered? Tens of thousands of people living in America today have asked themselves the same question when it comes to their loved ones.

Guns and a "cowboy mentality" seems to dominate American politics. Reasonable gun control seems no closer today than it was when children were murdered in schools across America. In today's America somewhere innocent people are dying on the streets.

In my hometown of Annapolis, Maryland with a population of about 40, 000 people and 4,000 of them midshipmen at the United States Naval Academy, violence reached an epidemic proportion. People in my hometown gave its police chief a "vote of no confidence".

They would later do the same thing to their mayor by ousting him out of office. If you ever attended a funeral of a young person who is in a casket, it represents the great failure of politicians. We elect people to public office to solve problems. These problems are not insurmountable, what they require is political will.

The National Rifle Association has a disproportionate grip on politics today. In the White House, they have an ally who has shown little empathy to the victims of these crimes.

I will never forget a meeting that I and others had with the mayor of Annapolis. We were at City Hall discussing racial issues. An aide came into the meeting and whispered something in the mayor's ear.

He excused himself and left out. A few minutes later he came and reported that there had been a shooting at the capitol. Annapolis is the capital of Maryland and we assumed that the shooting had occurred at the State House.

Minutes later, we discovered that a mass shooting had occurred at *The Capital-Gazette* newspaper and that five people were murdered. The journalists that were massacred were people we knew and in some cases, they were friends.

The murder at the newspaper underscored that the illicit use of guns by people had reached a new high. If a journalist could be murdered, who was safe?

Those journalists were murdered because of the assailant's belief that the newspaper had wronged him. It didn't matter that the writer of the story that infuriated him was no longer employed there.

To the assailant, the newspaper represented "fake news" and therefore the people who were employed there were worthy of death and were the enemy of the people. What is said out of the White House, I believe contributed to the violence.

Following is my opinion on guns and violence.

Carl Snowden: Police chief's decisions questionable

October 11, 2016

The Capital and other media outlets have reported on the record number of homicides in Annapolis – a record that has raised serious questions of leadership. What has not been reported is the growing frustration with the leadership of Chief Michael Pristoop. There is growing sentiment he is not providing the leadership necessary and our elected officials are overlooking his errors in managing the police department.

Chief Pristoop has been the leader of the police department for eight years. He has worked under three administrations and has been in law enforcement for 30 years. At $153,000 a year, he is the highest-paid official in our municipality. Citizens have every right to expect that their tax dollars be used prudently.

Some of his mistakes have resulted in him and the city being lampooned nationally by late-night comedians, as when he appeared before the General Assembly in 2014 and erroneously declared that 37 people had died of "an overdose" on the first day marijuana was legalized in Colorado. It was later learned Chief Pristoop acquired this fallacious data from a satirical website. He later apologized to the public and members of the General Assembly.

His decision not to attend the funeral of Annapolis police Detective Shelley C. White Sr., a 19-year veteran, was seen as another major mistake – one he never apologized for. Detective White – who, along with other Annapolis police officers, had alleged that systematic racism existed in the department – was a very popular police officer.

Earlier this year, at a meeting of the City Council's Public Safety Committee, Chief Pristoop actually defended the illegal altercation of an arrest warrant by an officer who was later promoted. Chief Pristoop is on record saying that knowing what he knows today, and even though a judge found the officer liable, he would do the same thing again. Incredible.

He also defended the promotion of an officer who admitted in a federal court deposition that she had falsified a police report. Again, no apologies were offered.

Recently, an African-American alderman informed the chief that a white police officer refused to speak to the alderman at Annapolis Police Department headquarters. The alderman said "Good morning" twice to the officer, who refused to acknowledge the greeting. This slight was captured on video and occurred in the presence of witnesses.

One can only wonder what that officer's behavior must be like to citizens who are not elected officials and who do not have the benefit of a video record. As of this writing, there is no indication Chief Pristoop took any steps to discipline the officer for his blatant disrespect to an elected official or to apologize to that official.

The Anne Arundel County NAACP and the Caucus of African-American Leaders have met with city officials to address racial disparities and made numerous recommendations for improvements. To date the City Council has passed one piece of legislation in this area – giving families of deceased police officers and firefighters the option of having an honor guard at the funerals. In addition, the mayor has hired a part-time African-American liaison and agreed to a pilot program involving the use of body cameras.

But there have been at least three additional complaints, alleging disparate treatment, filed with the federal Equal Employment Opportunity Commission.

The Caucus of African-American Leaders meets on the second Tuesday of each month at the Wiley H. Bates Legacy Center, 1101 Smithville St. in Annapolis. This meeting is open to the public as we continue to keep Dr. King's legacy alive.

Ultimately, taxpayers, voters and citizens, who must determine whether they are getting their money's worth from their public servants. Tonight, citizens will have an opportunity to express a vote of confidence or no confidence in their police chief. You are invited to express your views.

A Luta Continua, which means in Portuguese that the struggle continues.

Carl Snowden: Work remains on police, community relations

July 10, 2017

In many of the cities of our nation, we are facing a dichotomy: two phenomenon at the same time.

In Annapolis, Baltimore, Chicago and elsewhere we saw an unprecedented increase in homicides last year. Annapolitans were stunned to see the rise in murders. There were candlelight marches and vigils to focus attention on this issue.

Meanwhile, all over the nation, we have witnessed an increase in police-related shootings and other deaths. People like Sandra Bland, Freddie Gray, Michael Brown and Philando Castile became household names. These deaths all involved controversial actions by police. The acquittals of police officers in these cases remain a subject of dispute.

Some of these cases resulted in civil lawsuits being filed against municipalities. Baltimore and Chicago paid millions of dollars in settlements to the families of the deceased. The U.S. Department of Justice entered into consent decrees to improve police and community relations in those cities.

The Caucus of African-American Leaders and the local NAACP held a jam-packed town hall meeting at City Hall to look at ways that police-community relations could be improved at the local level. Now, a genuine effort is underway to improve that relationship.

Retired Baltimore County police Officer Sgt. Randy Williams and retired Annapolis police Lt. Robert E. Beans Sr. reviewed the situation and made numerous recommendations regarding the Annapolis Police Department's general orders. Some of those recommendations have been implemented and others are being reviewed by Chief Scott Baker and his command staff.

The Anne Arundel County Police Department under Chief Tim Altomare entered into an agreement with the Justice Department and they, too, are working diligently to improve police-community relations.

The recent fatal stabbing of 2nd Lt. Richard Wilbur Collins, allegedly by a Severna Park man with ties to a white supremacist group, underscored the need to improve race relations in our county. County Executive Steve Schuh will be meeting with members of the Caucus later this month to explain his administration's plan to do so.

At this evening's meeting of the Caucus of African-American Leaders, Neill Franklin, a retired state police officer, will be discussing the thought-provoking film "Walking Black," a documentary on how police-community relations can be improved. The meeting will begin at 5 at the Wiley H. Bates Legacy Center, 1101 Smithville St., Annapolis. It is open to the public.

The struggle for racial equality and justice continues. You can be a part of the solution or part of the problem. The choice is yours.

Carl Snowden: Help fund a memorial to slain Capital Gazette journalists

July 23, 2018

Earlier this month the Caucus of African-American Leaders and the Dr. Martin Luther King Jr. Committee, Inc. announced that they would spearhead a capital fundraising drive to raise $70,000 for a permanent memorial to the slain journalists who were murdered last month.

These martyrs: Gerald Fischman, Rob Hiassen, John McNamara, Rebecca Smith and Wendi Winters must never be forgotten. Here is why. The late CBS journalist Walter Cronkite once said, "Freedom of the press is not just important to democracy, it is democracy."

These journalists' lives were lost for a noble cause – freedom of the press. The proposed Freedom of the Press Memorial will be located within the City of Annapolis. Mayor Gavin Buckley has already assigned members of his staff to identify an appropriate location for the memorial. The site chosen will be accessible to the public.

I have heard from so many people including former Mayor Ellen O. Moyer all offered to assist with this project. Former Annapolis police Chief Joseph S. Johnson discussed the need for City Hall to review its security as well.

The night that the proposed memorial was announced, Leutrell Osborne, a retired CIA agent donated $100. Osborne knew that the men and women who were slain didn't represent fake news but men and women who were committed to factual news. He believed that they like his former colleagues they were committed to the principle of a democracy.

It is the same reason that Jeff Blum, whose father was the late Morris H. Blum founder of WANN radio made a contribution. As a former WANN radio journalist, Jeff Blum understood what this memorial represents.

The right to speak, publish and criticize the government is a right that most Americans cherished. It is one of the founding principles of this nation.

America has been and must always be a beacon of democracy and where people are able to express their views without the fear of being murdered for those views.

Anyone in the public eye can attest to the fact that the climate today is less civil and more corrosive than ever before. People do not just disagree they seek to silence their opponents. This is why the Freedom of the Press Memorial is so important. It is a memorial that says to every citizen and visitor that these journalists died for a noble cause.

In too many cases, tragedies are soon forgotten. This memorial will be the first of its kind in the nation to honor journalists who lost their lives because of a newspaper that published a story that the alleged assailant didn't like. If our society ever allowed this to become the norm, we will have lost more than the lives of these men and women, we would have lost our way.

The Dr. Martin Luther King, Jr. Committee, Inc., have built all of its memorials in the county from private funding. We raised the money and built the memorial to King at Anne Arundel Community College and donated it to the college. We did the same thing with the Civil Rights

Memorial, which is located across from the Arundel Center, which was donated to the City of Annapolis.

It is our intention to do the same thing with the Freedom of the Press Memorial, that is, donate it to the City of Annapolis. For readers who are interested in supporting the work of the Dr. Martin Luther King, Jr. Committee, Inc., they can make a tax-deductible contribution to www.mlkjrmd.org.

Thomas Jefferson once said, "Our liberty depends on freedom of the press, and that cannot be limited without being lost."

I simply say, *A Luta Continua*, which means in Portuguese that the struggle continues and that without freedom of the press, there is no freedom.

Carl Snowden: Thanking firefighters for their work in Capital Gazette shooting

August 06, 2018

I have always felt that civil servants are often taken for granted. Recently, the Caucus of African-American Leaders established branches in Baltimore County and Harford County.

Last week, we met with interim Baltimore County Executive Don Mohler. Mr. Mohler was running behind schedule. He told us that he was late because of a new practice that he had initiated.

He was going to various departments and thanking employees for their services. He had just returned from thanking public works employees particularly those who work on septic systems for their service during the floods that occurred in his county.

I know that there are those who say that is what they get paid for, yet, I believe it is important to thank people for doing their jobs during natural disasters and man-made ones.

Last month at our caucus meeting, we honored all of the members of the Anne Arundel and Annapolis police departments for the job they did when an active shooter murdered journalists at the Capital Gazette newsroom.

The weekend before this tragedy, Annapolis Deputy Fire Chief Kevin Simmons spearheaded an active shooting training exercise with public safety employees that made the front page of The Capital. Neither he nor the employees of that newspaper could have foreseen how important this training would be less than a week later.

On June 28, the law-enforcement personnel responded with professionalism and a level of sensitivity that we felt should be applauded. Some thought it was unusual for a civil rights organization to in this day and age to be honoring the police. The fact of the matter is the vast majority of citizens support law-enforcement when they enforce the law judiciously and without bias.

At the Caucus of African-American Leaders meeting Aug. 14, we will be honoring the firefighters and first responders of both the Anne Arundel County and Annapolis Fire Departments. We have invited County Executive Steve Schuh and Mayor Gavin Buckley or their designee to receive a plaque on behalf of their respective fire department.

On the infamous date of June 28, firefighters and first responders acted as a team. They made all of us proud. Their actions helped to save lives and restore order.

We have asked Mayor Gavin Buckley, County Executive Steve Schuh and Capital-Gazette Editor Rick Hutzell to be on hand to thank these men and women for their service to the community.

Civil servants have always held a special place in my heart. I am reminded that one of the last speeches that Martin Luther King, Jr. gave was to a group of sanitation workers in Memphis, Tennessee.

Many wondered why King, a Nobel Peace prize winner would spend his time with sanitation workers. King pointed out that all labor is important. He said that all labor has dignity and worth.

King said, "If it falls to your lot to be a street sweeper, sweep streets like Michelangelo painted pictures, sweep streets like Beethoven composed music…Sweep streets so well that all the hosts of heaven and earth will have to pause and say: Here lived a great street sweeper who swept his job well".

A Luta Continua, which means in Portuguese that the struggle continues.

Carl Snowden: Despite the shootings, goodness will triumph over evil

March 25, 2019

The headline read that "Over 50 Muslims were murdered by a self-avowed white supremacist in New Zealand." Those blaring headlines are becoming all too familiar.

Eleven Jews massacred in Pittsburgh at a synagogue, nine African-Americans killed at a black church in Charleston, South Carolina and five employees of the Capital-Gazette newspaper slaughtered in Annapolis.

Each of those mass killings generated headlines around the world and they brought freedom loving people to the frontlines.

Last week, citizens once again rallied at the Civil Rights Foot Soldiers Memorial across from the Arundel Center in Annapolis to demand an end to these senseless deaths. Five months earlier, they were at City Hall to call attention to the tragedy that had occurred in Pittsburgh.

Elected officials speaking at the rally at the Civil Rights Foot Soldiers Memorial, which was spearheaded by Yasemin Jamison, were U.S. Rep. John P. Sarbanes, County Executive Steuart Pittman and Mayor Gavin Buckley.

Other elected officials present included Delegates Alice Cain, Mike Rogers, Councilwoman Lisa Brannigan Rodvien and Orphans Court Judge Vickie Gipson. I listened intently as these speakers and others spoke passionately about mass shootings.

I was part of a generation that experienced the assassinations of NAACP leader Medgar Evers, President John F. Kennedy, Malcolm X, Dr. Martin Luther King, Jr., and Senator Robert F. Kennedy. Each of those assassinations shocked the nation.

Yet, today's mass killings of gays, students, journalists, Jews, Muslims and Christians no longer seem to have the same impact.

We now read about these events and their occurrences and are now so frequent that now they appear to be part of the body politic.

Our children and grandchildren are experiencing these mass killings at a level never before seen by any American generation.

A common denominator that all of these mass killings have is that they are aimed at people who are "different."

People with a different religion, different color, different sexual orientation, different race. Different. Ironically, America was founded on the principle that being "different" was OK.

Our Constitution allows us to practice or not to practice our religion of choice. We have the right in this nation to speak, criticize and petition our government officials.

I looked out at the children that were among the crowd of protestors and I thought about my grandchildren and how much different the world is that they are growing up in.

Americans truly have a choice to make, what kind of nation do we want to live in? Will it be a nation where mass killings are common or will we elect leaders to change the course of our nation?

By nature, I am an optimist. I believe in what Dr. King once said, "only when it gets dark enough, can you see the stars". Last week, I left that rally optimistic.

I was optimistic because despite the efforts of White Supremacists to divide us, people of goodwill, regardless of their religion, color, race or nationality, still believe in an America, in which people who are different are respected and protected.

I believe no matter how difficult the struggle is that in the final analysis goodness will triumph over evil and that the clarion call of *A Luta Continua*, which means in Portuguese that the struggle for a world of freedom, peace and justice for all humankind will prevail.

Carl Snowden: Annapolis public safety team should address continuing violence

August 12, 2019

Children often ask questions that begin with the word why? Why are there so many mass murders occurring in America? Why are so many people being murdered in Anne Arundel County and Baltimore City? Why haven't elected officials been able to address this problem? Why?

Last week, when the mass shootings occurred in Texas and Ohio, I immediately thought about the shootings that occurred at The Capital newspaper last year in Annapolis and our community's response. We held a candlelight vigil and a concert. We raised money for a memorial and scholarships.

When the murders occurred of Jews at the Tree of Life Synagogue in Pittsburgh, our community responded with a City Hall demonstration and candlelight vigil.

When the subsequent and senseless murders that have taken the lives of so many young local young people including Tre Da Kid, Elijah Wilson as a result of gun violence, we responded with prayers and a candlelight vigil. Somehow these acts of compassion and concerns did not answer our children's question.

Children who asked the questions, expect adults to have the answers and you may be surprised to learn that we do know how to prevent violence in our cities and societies. What we lack is the political will to do so.

When Mayor Gavin Buckley was elected to office, it came on the heels of record homicides in the City of Annapolis. People who were dying never had previous mayor or police chief attend their funerals.

Mayor Buckley's "One Annapolis" concept was both promising and new. During the mayoral election, candidates running for City Council pledged to support a new program modeled after Oakland, California's successful anti-violence program. It is called Oakland Unite.

Oakland Unite in partnership with the Youth Leadership Development and Civic Engagement has been able to literally make a difference in the lives of people. "All Oakland Unite's programs target Oakland's highest risk community members and neighborhoods, with a particular focus of interrupting violence now as it is occurring and preventing future violence."

The vast majority of members of the Annapolis City Council pledged their support for this initiative during the campaign.

In fact, Alderwoman Rhonda Pindell Charles, chair of the City Council's Public Safety Committee drafted legislation, which was never introduced. Buckley agreed to sign on to the legislation but didn't include it in either of his budgets. Children ask simple questions why?

Last week, many houses of worship, churches, synagogues, mosques, and temples received information entitled "Keeping Your House of Worship Safe" from the City's Office of Emergency Management(OEM).

Last week, a new police chief, fire chief, and emergency management director were unanimously approved by the City Council. They were called the "new" Public Safety Team. How does the "new" team plan to answer the question that children have been asking?

At 6 p.m. Tuesday, we have invited Annapolis Police Chief Ed Jackson, Fire Chief Doug Remaley and OEM Director Kevin Simmons to address the Caucus of African-American Leaders at the Wiley H. Bates Community Room, 1101 Smithville St, Annapolis. This meeting is open to the public and a complimentary dinner will be served at 5:00 p.m courtesy of Alderman DaJuan Gay. Attendees will have an opportunity to ask questions.

One of the things that I know is that we must not allow it to become normal for journalists to be killed, houses of worship and shopping centers to be targeted and young people to be murdered in our county. Children who asked the question "why?" deserves better answers than the adults have been giving them and I for one, refuse to accept the notion that this is the new America.

A Luta Continua, which means in Portuguese that the struggle continues.

Carl Snowden: Pause today to remember a day that briefly united America

September 11, 2018

There are some anniversaries that you remember exactly what you were doing when the event occured. I remember what I was doing when President John F. Kennedy, Malcolm X, Senator Robert F. Kennedy and Martin Luther King, Jr. were assassinated. These murders left an indelible mark on my psyche.

However, there is another horrific event that changed forever our nation. I know exactly where I was and what I was doing on Sept. 11, 2001.

I was a member of the then-county executive Janet S. Owens' cabinet. Owens had become the first woman elected as county executive. She had been in office for three years. I had taken the day off to campaign for Ellen Moyer, who was running to become the first Annapolis female mayor.

I was in the Robinwood community passing out literature and a little boy came running up to me and breathlessly proclaimed, "America is under attack." He then said, "it's on television" before he dashed away.

America would never be the same again. I remember President George W. Bush standing in the rubble in New York City with the bullhorn. I remember being a part of a task force that looked at the vulnerability of Anne Arundel County to terrorist attacks.

Everything and everybody was affected by this attack. I remember Owens calling on us to unite as a community in the face of this attack. I remember how people regardless of their race, religion, nationality or gender stood united.

When you contrast that moment with today, it is clear that the unity that once prevailed in our nation is no more. We recently witnessed this with the funerals of Aretha Franklin and Sen. John McCain. We know that Congress is divided and that we have a president who tweets more than he unites people.

On this anniversary of 911, our democracy, and its institutions are being challenged as never before. Yet, it is not a foreign power that threatens our democracy, it is a Congress that has failed to hear the words of McCain, who warned them to put democratic principles before party.

It is a president that from the day he took office, has never adhered to Franklin's anthem of "Respect."

There are many children today who were born after Sept. 11, 2001, and they didn't witness America's ability to put aside our ideological differences and look at the things that unite us.

The Caucus of African-American Leaders recently has been honoring firefighters, police officers and first responders for their response to the mass shooting that occurred at The Capital newspaper on June 28.

There have been those who wondered why. It is because like the attack 17 years ago, it was not on individuals, but, an attack on all Americans.

When journalists are murdered for doing their jobs, it is an attack on the First Amendment and the principles that we hold dear. It is an attack on our democracy.

I have never brought into the misguided mantra that the "press is an enemy of the people." This wrong-headed assertion must never become the rallying cry for despots, who seek to silence dissent and stifle freedom. We must be united in our opposition to silence the media.

We will remember that America with all of its imperfections, is humanity's best hope for the world. We will once again, pause to thank the men and women who every day seek to protect us. We will pause to remember the journalists who lost their lives to senseless violence.

On this day, on this infamous anniversary, *A Luta Continua*, which means in Portuguese that the struggle for a more inclusive and united community is more important than ever before.

Let us pray that the next time someone says "America is under attack" it will not be Americans who are doing the attacking.

WOMEN

Caucus of African-American Leaders celebrates Women History Month 2019

The contributions that women have made to our society and the world have long been overlooked. Even today, women have been denied their rightful place in history. I have written columns on the need for "her-story" and not just "his-story".

I am privileged at the time of this writing to have a mother who is a 104 years old. This chapter on women is written with her mind. She was born in 1916 before women had the right to vote.

As a black woman, she had to carry the burden of both sexism and racism. Over the years I have met and admired strong women. When I was a teenager I met Congresswoman Shirley Chisholm. I watched Coretta Scott King and Betty Shabazz raised their children after their fathers had been murdered.

I admired Maya Angelou and Nikki Giovanni for their wisdom and poetry. I have known Annapolis women like Elizamae Robinson, Bertina Nick, Vicky Bruce, Monica Lindsey, and countless others.

Years ago, we started the Fannie Lou Hamer Reception held at St. John's College to highlight the contributions of all women. We wanted to ensure that women who were nondescript and those who are well-known were honored at an annual award's reception.

This chapter is dedicated to women who through sheer audacity and tenacity demand that little girls' horizons only be limited by their God-given talents.

Carl Snowden: Proposed memorial would honor pathbreakers

March 24, 2015

The recent announcement by U.S. Sen. Barbara A. Mikulski that she will be retiring at the end of her term left many of us wondering how best to honor her. Ironically, the announcement came during Women's History Month.

Women's History Month, like Black History Month, allows us to pause and measure the progress that we have made as a society. During this month I often think of my mother, who was born in 1917 and is 98 years old. In her lifetime, she has had to deal with both racism and sexism.

Sen. Mikulski's retirement takes on a different meaning for her. When she was born, women could not vote and African-Americans lived under an apartheid system that segregated them according to their color and race. In her almost one century of living, she has seen America through a prism that many have not.

Her wisdom is what I rely on. I wanted to find out from her how we should honor the retiring U.S. senator. She has always admired Sen. Mikulski and so have I.

My mother's response was that we must educate generations unborn about the struggle for equality and moving our nation toward a more perfect union. She recommended that we do a memorial that reflected the progress that Maryland has made in promoting racial and gender equality.

After meeting with members of the Dr. Martin Luther King Jr. Committee Inc., which I chair, we have decided to build one final memorial that will encompass my mother's recommendation.

The memorial would be dedicated to two great Marylanders; the late U.S. Rep. Parren J. Mitchell and U.S. Sen. Barbara A. Mikulski. These two history-makers symbolize the great progress that we have made in our nation and state.

Congressman Mitchell was the first African-American elected from the state of Maryland to the U.S. House of Representatives. Sen. Mikulski was the first woman elected from our state and the longest-serving female in the history of the nation to serve in the U.S. Senate.

These two outstanding public servants have left a great legacy. I had the privileged of working with both of them over the years on social justice issues. Their achievements remind me of how far we have come.

I have discussed this project with House of Delegates Speaker Michael Busch, former County Councilman Daryl Jones, Alderman Joe Budge and other elected officials. If the family of Rep. Mitchell and Sen. Mikulski concur, we will build this memorial prior to Sen. Mikulski's retirement.

We will launch a capital fundraising campaign this fall entitled "Maryland's First," raise money privately and then donate the memorial to an appropriate governmental or educational entity.

I am proud of the fact that all of the previous memorials that we have built have been done through generous contributions of citizens throughout the state of Maryland. Once getting the aforementioned permission of the Mitchell and Mikulski representatives, we will begin the process.

When my mother was born, women could not vote and an African-American president did not exist. During Women's History Month not only does my mother see a different America, my granddaughters are able to live the American dream because of a woman name Barbara Mikulski, whom neither knew — but if this memorial is built, neither they, nor countless children, will ever forget her.

A Luta Continua, which means the struggle continues.

Carl Snowden: Fannie Lou Hamer left huge legacy

September 22, 2015

Anne Arundel County is the only jurisdiction in Maryland to recognize the birthday of the late Mississippi feminist and civil rights heroine Fannie Lou Hamer by honoring women from different racial backgrounds. We Marylanders have been celebrating the birthday and legacy of this Mississippian for two decades. Why do we celebrate her birth?

Mrs. Hamer was born on Oct. 6, 1917, into a society in which neither women nor African-Americans were permitted to exercise their right to vote.

Mrs. Hamer, a sharecropper, is not a household name like her more famous contemporaries Lady Bird Johnson, Coretta Scott King, Jackie Kennedy and Rosa Parks. Yet she arguably did more to advance voting rights in this nation than anyone else. Her 1964 speech before the Democratic National Convention was the catalyst for the passage in 1965 of the historic Voting Rights Act signed into law by President Lyndon Baines Johnson.

Mrs. Hamer epitomized the women who were the backbone of the civil rights movement. She represented the thousands of nameless women and men who were the foot soldiers of the civil rights movement. They often did not even get a footnote in our history books.

The movement's leadership was dominated by men. Yet, astute observers know it was women like Mrs. Hamer who were in the forefront in demonstrating courage and conviction.

She was brutally beaten while in jail on trumped-up charges that were later dismissed. Fresh out a jail cell, bruised and injured, she nevertheless came to a voting rights rally in Mississippi and told the audience that she was going to take people to register to vote.

She was only 5 feet 4 inches, yet she once stated, "But if I fail, I'll fall five feet four inches forward in the fight for freedom. I'm not backing off." This is the kind of courage that must never be forgotten.

Two decades ago, we decided to hold an annual Fannie Lou Hamer Reception to honor women who, like Mrs. Hamer, are making a difference in the lives of their fellow citizens. We pause on the eve of her birthday annually to honor women and to remind Marylanders of her role in making democracy a reality for millions of Americans.

Some past honorees you will recognize: U.S. Sen. Barbara Mikulski, former County Executive Janet Owens, former Mayor Ellen O. Moyer, former Del. Mary Ann Love, Alderwoman Sheila Finlayson, Christine Davenport, Judge Michele Jaklitsch, Alderwoman Cynthia Carter, Janice Hayes-Williams, the Rev. Mamie Williams, Dr. Charlestine Fairley, Edith Knight and Judge Cathy Vitale — to name just a few.

Others, like the Rev. Diane Dixon Proctor, Minister Ann Davis, Mary DesChamps, Lisa Ennis, Karen Slade and Dawn Lindsay — this year's recipients — are not elected officials, but, like Mrs. Hamer, have made a huge contribution to the community.

At 4 p.m. Oct. 4 at the Francis Key Auditorium of St. John's College, in honor of the 20th anniversary of the Fannie Lou Hamer awards, all of the previous recipients will be recognized.

Admission is $35 per person, and tickets may be purchased at the door on the day of the event. Proceeds will go toward the maintenance and upkeep of the Civil Rights Foot Soldiers Memorial.

If you know of a previous Fannie Lou Hamer award recipient, please have her attend this reception. A documentary on the life of Mrs. Hamer will be shown.

Mrs. Hamer is known for her famous quotes — "I am sick and tired of being sick and tired," and "People have to get together and work together." However, Mrs. Hamer once said that "When we women make up our minds to change the world, it will change."

Thanks to Mrs. Hamer and the women we are honoring, the world is changing.

A Luta Continua, which in Portuguese means "the struggle continues."

Carl Snowden: Oprah knew the future is always in our hands

October 27, 2015

Years ago, I worked with Oprah Winfrey at WJZ-TV in Baltimore. The native of Mississippi was just getting her start and she was very personable.

I was working at the television station as a commentator for their WJZ-TV's public affairs program, "Sunday Live" and was a panelist for the "Square-Off" program.

While at that Baltimore television station, Oprah did a number of community events. She spoke at a rally at the 200-family public housing community called Meade Village in Severn, MD.

At that time the community was facing many challenges. The issues then were similar to those today: systemic racism, poverty, income inequality, drugs, illicit guns and apathy.

Oprah being a celebrity, we hoped she would draw a large crowd — and she did. After giving some brief introductory remarks, I turned the microphone over to her. What she told that predominantly African-American audience is as true today as it was then.

She told the following story: There were two little boys who were mischievous and looking for someone to play a prank on. They saw an old man. One little boy said to the other, "Let's trick this old man."

"How?" said the other.

"Let's catch a bird," said his friend. He explained that they would ask the old man, "Is the bird alive or is it dead?" If the old man answered that it was alive, they would crush it. If the old man answered that the bird is dead, they would allow it to fly away.

The boys believed they had come up with the perfect prank. They caught a bird and concealed it in their hands.

Giggling, they approached the old man and said, "Old man, we have a bird in our hands. Is the bird alive or is it dead?"

[The old man, without hesitation, looked at the boys and said, "It's in your hands," then walked away.

Oprah Winfrey told her low-income public housing audience that day, that the future of their community and the future of their children was in their hands.

I have never forgotten that story. Its truth transcends time and circumstances. We collectively have the power to change our conditions.

A determined people can take adversity and transform a stumbling block into a steppingstone. People who understand that it is not where you begin in life but where you end know about the most important aspect of anyone's journey.

Oprah Winfrey, now a billionaire, has been all over the world. It is doubtful she even remembers visiting Meade Village, yet every time, I see her on television, I think about those little boys asking, "Old man, is the bird in our hands alive or dead?" and his wise response, "It's in your hands."

A Luta Continua, which in Portuguese means that the struggle continues.

Carl Snowden: Elizamae Robinson: An unsung heroine

January 26, 2016

Earlier this month we celebrated the birthday of Dr. Martin Luther King Jr. and heard Baltimore City's state's attorney call on citizens to move from apathy to action.

Marilyn Mosby did not get an opportunity to meet an Annapolitan who not only reflected the spirit of activism that she was exhorting this generation to take up, but made history in the process.

Today I want to pay tribute to an unsung heroine, Elizamae Robinson. Mrs. Robinson was appointed by former Mayor Josh Cohen to the Housing Authority of the City of Annapolis board of commissioners and is a member of First Baptist Church.

This unassuming woman has a history of activism that many will be surprised to learn. She helped to organize the longest rent strike in the history of Maryland — one that lasted more than 18 months.

As a former resident of the subsidized Ken-Marr Apartments (now known as Woodside Gardens) in the 1970s, she helped to organize her neighbors to protest the slum-like conditions that once existed in that community.

She took on a former management company and the U.S. Department of Housing and Urban Development, without collywobbles, and won!

Ask local attorney Alan H. Legum, who represented her and other tenants, and he will tell you that she was a tenacious litigant and one of the most articulate advocates for affordable housing that he ever met. Her position was that residents had a right to live in decent and affordable housing.

She placed her rent into an escrow fund, as did her neighbors, and refused to pay rent until the conditions in her community were improved.

She participated in marches, attended City Council meetings and demanded that her community be treated with respect. State's Attorney Mosby would be proud of her. They do not make them like that anymore.

Now 83, a grandmother and great-grandmother, she epitomizes the women who exist in our community. She is someone who is not a household name, but made a big difference in the lives of people.

The HACA board of commissioners unanimously named the Newtowne 20 Community Center, adjacent to Woodside Gardens, in her honor. Both Woodside Gardens and Newtowne 20 will undergo renovations in the years to come and a new Elizamae Robinson Community Center will be built.

One of my favorite pastimes was to visit her at her home in Ken-Marr Apartments on a Saturday afternoon. In her home she would have on WPFW radio and we would listen to two great radio personalities: Jerry "The Bama" Washington and Billy Ray.

Chicken would be frying and the late community activist Bertina Nick would be sitting at the table with Charles "Fatmeat" Gray, Jeff Henderson, James Chase, Wendy Hinton and others discussing current events and politics.

Also, Mrs. Robinson at the time ran a candy store, patronized by children and adults. She would greet each one with a smile and a word of encouragement. They knew her and she knew each of them either by their first name or their family.

Looking back on those Saturday afternoons, I will always treasure them: great food, great music, great conversations and great friendships. Her personality is the perfect intenerate.

It is not often that people get to meet living history. If you ever run into her, just tip your hat and know that Annapolis produced one of the finest organizers Maryland has ever seen — and if you don't believe it, ask any HUD official.

A Luta Continua, which, in Portuguese, means that the struggle continues.

Carl Snowden: Dorothy Height had a lasting impact

August 09, 2016

It is said that when you throw a pebble into the water, it creates a rippling effect. Most people think that when they can no longer see the ripples, the pebble's effect has come to an end.

Oh, how wrong they are!

If they ever had the opportunity to meet the late Dr. Dorothy Irene Height, they would know that, like the pebbles tossed in the water, her influence on the events of our time is eternal.

Height knew both Martin Luther King Jr. and Malcolm X. She knew presidents and first ladies. She was an incredible woman. She was known for her stylish hats, which often were coordinated with her dresses and handbags.

When people could not remember her name, they would refer to her as the "woman in the hat." What I most admired about her was her uncanny ability to see the potential in young women and guide them to places they could not have dreamed of.

A proponent of education, she often counseled women to get their college degrees. She held several degrees herself and was the recipient of many honorary degrees from major colleges and universities.

I have met so many successful women over the years, who speak her name with reverence. Imagine a woman who had dined with first lady Eleanor Roosevelt, danced with Maya Angelou, marched with Rosa Parks and called Coretta Scott King her "sister." She knew the famous and the nondescript.

Years ago, she advocated for a black family reunion every year in Washington, D.C., a reunion that continues to this day. She believed in women rights and civil rights.

During her lifetime, she participated in major demonstration that occurred from the 1963 March on Washington to the 1995 Million Man March.

A feminist before the term became chic, she never saw the role of women as being subordinate to men, but, rather full and equal partners.

A woman whose ego was never challenged by the success of others, but, rather she celebrated their successes.

The Rev. Mamie Williams and Pastor Zina Pierre are just two local women, whose lives were impacted by her friendship and mentorship.

Pierre served in the Clinton administration and Williams became a district superintendent for the Baltimore-Washington Conference of the United Methodist Church.

Height died at the age of 98, but her impact, like that pebble on the water, continues. If you don't believe me, just ask anybody who ever met her and they will tell you she left a lasting impact on them — the ripples continues.

A Luta Continua, which means, in Portuguese, "the struggle continues."

Carl Snowden: Hamer award winners make a difference

September 27, 2016

Why have Marylanders for more than two decades honored a Mississippi sharecropper? Why is Anne Arundel County the only jurisdiction that honors a feminist and civil rights heroine — a woman whose stentorian voice was almost lost in our history books?

Fannie Lou Hamer was born on Oct. 6, 1917, into a society in which neither women nor African-Americans were permitted to exercise their right to vote in an American democracy. Mrs. Hamer was determined to change that.

Through fierce determination, her advocacy contributed to the passage of the historic 1965 Voting Rights Act by Congress.

This federal law is credited with creating an opportunity that led to tens of thousands of African-Americans, Latinos and women being elected to public offices which where never held before by women and people of color.

Indeed, if it had not been for Mrs. Hamer, it is unlikely there would have been a President Barrack Obama in the White House or a Barbara A. Mikulski in the U.S. Senate.

Mrs. Hamer, in the words of the Rev. Jesse Jackson, made it possible "for hands that once picked cotton to pick a president."

Yet many of our citizens have no idea who Mrs. Hamer was. Unlike her more famous contemporaries Malcolm X, Rosa Parks, Coretta Scott King or U.S. Sen. Robert F. Kennedy, hers is not a household name.

Still, she represents the backbone of the thousands of nameless people who were nondescript and yet made it possible for the voting rights that so many enjoy today.

These men and women were the backbone of the civil rights movement. They were the foot soldiers, who often did not even receive a footnote in our history books — ordinary men and women who made an extraordinary contribution to America.

Years ago in Anne Arundel County, we decided to hold an annual Fannie Lou Hamer Reception in her memory and honor women of various racial backgrounds who, like Mrs. Hamer, are making a difference in the lives of their fellow citizens.

Just this year, the General Assembly passed legislation that restored voting rights to thousands of citizens. This is the same legislature that in 1909 disenfranchised thousands of African-Americans with the infamous "grandfather law," which simply said that if your grandfather couldn't vote, then neither could you.

As a result of that law, no African-Americans were able to serve on the Annapolis City Council from 1906 until 1915, when the U.S. Supreme Court overturned the law.

At 4 p.m. Sunday at Francis Scott Key Auditorium of St. John's College, 60 College Ave., Annapolis, we will be honoring six local women at the 21st Annual Fannie Lou Hamer Reception. Like Mrs. Hamer, they may not be household names, but, they have made a difference in our county.

They are Paula J. Peters, Scotti Preston, Gordenia "Deni" Henson, Kashonna J. Holland, Marthena Speer Cowart and Sandra Wallace. These women, in their respective fields, have contributed to our county.

For more information, you can visit www.mlkjrmd.org.

Proceeds from the event will be used to pay off the debt incurred in building the Civil Rights Foot Soldiers Memorial in Whitmore Park, across from the Arundel Center.

Fannie Lou Hamer once observed that when "we women make up our minds to change the world, it will change" and that is precisely what our honorees have been doing: changing the world.

Chris Nelson, the retiring president of St. John's College, will receive the first Alan Hilliard Legum Civil Rights Award, named in honor of the late Annapolis civil rights attorney Alan Legum.

Mr. Nelson has been a staunch supporter of this event for more than a decade.

A Luta Continua, which in Portuguese means that "the struggle continues."

Carl Snowden: Remember what we owe to our grandmothers

December 13, 2016

One of my favorite Bill Withers songs is "Grandma's Hand's." I love this song because it so accurately reflects the women I know who have become grandmothers.

Some people watch clocks, I watch people. You can learn a great deal from watching people. For almost eight years, I have been watching Marian Shields Robinson. Most people will not recognize her or her name. Yet, she has played a pivotal role in the White House.

She is the mother of first lady Michelle Obama and the mother-in-law of President Barack Obama, but, more importantly, she is the grandmother of their children.

Grandmothers play such a vital role in the lives of their children and grandchildren. They are the "living history." They knew you when you were a child; also, they know you as an adult.

They bring a wisdom that only a grandmother can have. They are the ones who know what it is like to be "in love." They are the ones who recognize whether a prospective spouse is "good" or "bad" for you.

They have seen so much in their lifetimes. They see you in your children. They see themselves in you.

I have watched Mrs. Robinson from afar and have admired her greatly. She does not seek the limelight, but every time I have seen her with the president, the first lady or her grandchildren I immediately feel a sense of great pride.

Mrs. Robinson will be 80 years old next year. For me she represents all of those praying black grandmothers that I have met in my life — those grandmothers who were maids, who scrubbed floors and pinched pennies so that their children and grandchildren would have opportunities that they did not.

Those grandmothers who often said to their children, "Get a good education. It is the one thing that they can not take from you."

As those grandmothers have gotten older, their hands are no longer used for scrubbing floors and shaking a finger as they issue warnings. They are now used to pray. At night, in the stillness of the evening, you can hear them praying for their children and grandchildren.

On any Sunday, at any church, you can see them praying — praying for a better tomorrow. No one will ever know how many times they asked for God's intervention into the affairs of humankind.

I know how fortunate I am to have a mother who is 100 and continues to pray for her grandchildren. I can only imagine what it must feel like for Michelle to have both her children and her mother with them in the White House.

History books often do not detail the role that grandmothers play in the lives of the famous. That is why, as the Obamas prepare to leave the White House in January, their legacy will be found in a woman whose prayers were answered.

If you get an opportunity to listen to Bill Withers' "Grandma's Hand's, pay attention to these inspiring and enlightening lyrics:

Baby, Grandma understands that you love that man.

Put yourself in Jesus' hands.

Grandma's hands.

This evening at the monthly Caucus of African-American Leaders meeting at 6 at the Wiley H. Bates Legacy Center, 1101 Smithville St., Annapolis, we will pay a special tribute to Marian Shields Robinson, whose only title while at the White House was "Grandma" — and, as far as I am concerned, it is the greatest title she could have had. The meeting is open to the public.

A Luta Continua, which in Portuguese means that the struggle continues!

Carl Snowden: History must include 'her-story'

March 13, 2017

In 1987, the 100th Congress passed legislation designating March as Women's History Month. This year we are celebrating the 30th anniversary of this important recognition.

The legislation acknowledged that American history was largely being told as "his-story" and will never be accurate or complete without the "her-story" being told.

Women have made contributions in every field. In Maryland, former U.S. Sen. Barbara A. Mikulski became the longest-serving female in the history of the U.S. Senate. In Anne Arundel County the late Sarah Carter became the first and only African-American female to serve on the County Council. The late Alderwoman Barbara Neustadt and former Alderwoman Cynthia Carter were the first woman and first African-American woman, respectively, to serve on the Annapolis City Council.

Former U.S. Rep. Marjorie S. Holt, Anne Arundel County Executive Janet S. Owens and Annapolis Mayor Ellen O. Moyer and are the only women elected to their respective offices. Former U.S. Rep. Donna F. Edwards is the only African-American woman elected from Maryland to serve in the House of Representatives. Her district included a sliver of Anne Arundel County.

These former public servants' contributions have been immense, both to our community and our country. It is so important we honor women who have made a difference.

Every October, the Dr. Martin Luther King, Jr. Committee Inc. partners with St. John's College to honor women with the prestigious Fannie Lou Hamer Awards, named after the feminist and civil rights heroine. The award seeks to honor women of different racial backgrounds. For more than two decades women who are household names and women in charge of their households have received this award.

Recipients have included Charlestine R. Fairley, Juanita Cage Lewis, Felecia Carroll, former Alderwoman Classie Hoyle, Judge Pamela North, Alderwoman Sheila Finlayson, Alderwoman Rhonda Pindell-Charles, Polly Peters, Marthena Speer Cowart, Kathleen Nieberding Temprine and Gordenia "Deni" Henson, to name just a few. Their contributions have been in politics, law, banking, government, education, business, labor, arts, science and sports.

Congress made a wise decision in creating Women's History Month. It allows the nation to look at the contributions women have made over the years. Can you imagine an America that did not have the courage of a Rosa Parks? A nation that did not have the political contributions of former Texas Gov. Ann Richards or U.S. Rep. Barbara Jordan?

Anyone who knows the history of Betty Shabazz, Coretta Scott King, and first lady Jacqueline Kennedy — the widows of Malcolm X, the Rev. Martin Luther King Jr. and President John F. Kennedy, respectively — marveled at their grace during some of America's darkest moments.

An American history text book that does not include a Justice Sandra O'Connor, U.S. Rep. Shirley Chisholm, Harriet Tubman, Sojourner Truth, Eleanor Roosevelt, Billie Holiday or Michelle Obama is a textbook that will not educate our students to the rich contributions that women have made.

I am a firm believer we should recognize and celebrate the accomplishments of women in our nation. My mom, who is 101 years old, has seen many changes in our nation. Born in 1916, when women did not have the right to vote and African-Americans were disenfranchised, she has seen firsthand the progress women have made. Yet I am sure my mother would be the first to say that while women have come a long way, they have not reached their zenith.

Today at 5 p.m. at the monthly Caucus of African-American Leaders meeting at the Wiley H. Bates Legacy Center, 1101 Smithville St., Annapolis, we will pause during our social hour to pay tribute to women. Our regular meeting will begin at 6 p.m. This meeting is open to the public and all are welcome.

A Luta Continua, which in Portuguese means that the struggle continues for equality for women.

Carl Snowden: Mitchell and Holt should be honored

April 24, 2017

Former Anne Arundel County Councilman Daryl Jones recently wrote to Gov. Larry Hogan asking if there are any plans to name a state park, highway or building after the late U.S. Rep. Parren J. Mitchell, Maryland's first African-American congressman.

Mr. Mitchell was elected in 1971 and served for 16 years. He was the chairman and one of the founders of the Congressional Black Caucus. His oratorical skills won him national acclaim.

Mr. Jones' inquiry triggered a thought. Why isn't there more effort to preserve our history? As an eyewitness to that history, I am amazed by how few people understand the importance of preserving it.

I thought about former U.S. Rep. Marjorie S. Holt, who served with Mr. Mitchell. In 1973, she became the first woman elected from Anne Arundel County to the U.S. House of Representatives, where she served for 14 years.

During those years, I sought her assistance on many issues. She helped me and others preserve Bloomsbury Square, a public housing development in Annapolis that the state had threatened to demolish.

U.S. Reps. Holt and Mitchell assisted me in my efforts to stop the FBI from illegally spying on citizens in Anne Arundel during the 1970s.

I have letters that U.S. Rep. Holt wrote to federal officials decrying their unconstitutional surveillance of her constituents — surveillance a federal judge ordered to cease and desist immediately. These two history makers should not be forgotten.

It is my hope Gov. Hogan will find some appropriate way of honoring U.S. Rep. Mitchell.

I also think County Executive Steve Schuh should honor Mrs. Holt, who was the first Republican woman elected to Congress from Maryland.

While Mrs. Holt and I did not always agree on the issues, she had one of the best constituency offices I had ever seen. In fact, when I was elected to the Annapolis City Council, I emulated her when it came to constituency service — i.e., responding to every letter and returning every telephone call. During my 12 years of service as an elected official, I made it a point to work with both political parties.

Mrs. Holt, believed in the principle that once one is elected to office, you must represent all of your constituency, regardless of their political party, gender or race. Unfortunately, this concept is lost on too many of our elected representatives today.

Mrs. Holt believed in civil discourse. During her entire time in Congress, I had never heard her utter a disparaging remark about any of her colleagues.

Mr. Schuh should find some appropriate way to honor Mrs. Holt, by naming a county building in her honor or with some other appropriate recognition.

Mr. Jones and others are not waiting for the government to act to honor the memory of Mr. Mitchell. At the 7 p.m. Friday meeting of the West County Democratic Club of Anne Arundel

County, they will host its annual Parren J. Mitchell Dinner and Salute at Club Meade at Fort Meade. Tickets will be available at the door.

The dinner will be keynoted by nationally syndicated radio personality Joe Madison, known as the "Black Eagle." Mr. Madison's insightful analysis of events and appreciation for the work of the late Mr. Mitchell will be on full display.

Few citizens realize Mr. Mitchell was a Purple Heart recipient, recognized by the legendary General George S. Patton for his service.

It is my hope Messrs. Hogan and Schuh will honor these two public servants, who represented a generation more concerned about future generations than their next election.

They were truly public servants, as I knew from personal experience. I was privileged to call them my advocates for social justice.

Carl Snowden: Hamer awards honor heroine of civil rights movement

December 26, 2017

At 4 p.m. on Sunday at St. John's College's Francis Scott Key Auditorium, 60 College Ave. in Annapolis, six women will be awarded the prestigious Fannie Lou Hamer Award.

The newly inaugurated Alan Hillard Legum Civil Rights Award will also be given.

Mrs. Hamer was a feminist and a civil rights heroine. Unlike her better-known contemporaries — Rosa Parks, Betty Shabazz, Maya Angelou, Coretta Scott King, Janis Joplin and others — Mrs. Hamer was one of the foot soldiers of the civil rights movement.

This Mississippi sharecropper who wore flannel dresses and spoke plainly about the racism of her day was an incredible woman. She was severely beaten by black men at the orders of white law-enforcement officers, who wanted to punish her for her desire to register and vote.

When Mrs. Hamer told her story to a national television audience in 1964, she did something that even the Rev. Martin Luther King Jr. could not do — she described in vivid detail what it was like to be poor and black in Mississippi.

Her famous statement, "I am sick and tired of being sick and tired," resonated with Americans as no other testimony had and was the catalyst for Congress passing the historic 1965 Voting Rights Act.

More than two decades ago, the Dr. Martin Luther King Jr. Committee partnered with St. John's College to honor the memory of Mrs. Hamer on her birthday by giving awards to women from various racial backgrounds who were making a difference in Anne Arundel County.

Like Mrs. Hamer, these women were not necessarily household names. But, like Mrs. Hamer, they were making a difference in their community.

This Sunday, St. John's College President Panayiotis Kanelos will present Fannie Lou Hamer Awards to Sarah Elfreth, Yasemin Jamison, Yvette Jackson Morrow, MiaLissa Lynn Thompkins, Debbie Ritchie and Lisa DeJesus.

These women live and work in various parts of our county including Arnold, Severn, Annapolis, Pasadena and Edgewater. They have made a significant contribution to their communities.

Proceeds from this event will go toward retiring the debt incurred in building the first and only Civil Rights Foot Soldiers Memorial in the state of Maryland. The memorial is across from the Arundel Center and includes Mrs. Hamer's name. She died in 1977; this October marks the centennial of her birth.

She was once asked by Malcolm X if she prayed. Her response: "You can pray until you faint, but unless you get up and try to do something, God is not going to put it in your lap."

It was that plain spoken manner that made her a hero to so many. It is the reason Marylanders have paused on the eve of her birthday for 22 years to remind people that it is the foot soldiers who leave footprints in history. These footprints are often made by nondescript people who are not even footnotes in our history books.

It is the reason Marylanders each year celebrate the birthday of a Mississippi sharecropper because, in the final analysis, it is not what you do for a living, it is what you do to improve the lives of your fellow citizens.

It is also the reason that this column always ends with *A Luta Continua*, which means in Portuguese that the struggle continues for peace, equality and justice.

Carl Snowden: Area has had many women pathbreakers

March 12, 2018

Women's History Month is being celebrated throughout the nation. I and my mom, who is 102 years old, have both been eyewitnesses to history.

Prior to 1920, women were denied the right to vote. Contrast that to today. As of last month a record number of women had filed for elective offices in Anne Arundel County. Women are seeking a host of elective offices, including those of judge, state senator, delegate, county councilman and sheriff — the last of which has never been held by a woman.

Twenty years ago, I was part of the effort to elect Janet S. Owens as our first female county executive. I will never forget that race. Mrs. Owens defied the odds and won against a well-financed Republican incumbent. Her election was a watershed moment in our history.

There have been other watershed moments, including the election of former Mayor Ellen O. Moyer as the first female chief executive of Annapolis and that of Sarah Carter as the first African-American female member of our County Council.

I fondly remember the election of Alderwoman Barbara Neustadt, who in 1973 became the first woman on the Annapolis City Council. In 1997, Cynthia Abney Carter became the council's first African-American woman. I remember when Mary Sellman Jackson became the first African-American woman to be a judge of the county Orphans Court.

Over the years, I had the pleasure of working with former U.S. Sen. Barbara A. Mikulski and former U.S. Reps. Marjorie S. Holt and Donna Edwards, all of whom made history.

Sen. Mikulski was the longest-serving female in the history of the U.S. Senate. Mrs. Holt was the first female congresswoman from Anne Arundel County; Ms. Edwards was, to date, the only female African-American Maryland has sent to the House.

The inclusion of women has brought us not only talented leaders but problem-solvers as well.

Under Mrs. Owens' leadership, the Wiley H. Bates Heritage Center was finally renovated and completed and the Dr. Martin Luther King Jr. Memorial at Anne Arundel Community College came into existence. The Alex Haley-Kunta Kinte Memorial at City Dock was completed during the Moyer and Owens administrations.

When former Alderwoman Classie G. Hoyle was elected to the City Council, she changed the City Charter so that women on the council are called "alderwomen" rather than "aldermen."

Women like Delegate Mary Ann Love, Delegate Virginia Claggett, County Council member Ann Stockett and Alderwoman Ruth Gray made significant contributions to breaking glass ceilings.

And I'm convinced that this year Gov. Larry Hogan will appoint a woman of color to the Anne Arundel County Circuit Court, ending more than 367 years of exclusion. As many Capital readers realize, no Asians, Latinos, Native Americans or African-American women have ever served on this court. Last summer there were demonstrations protesting this exclusion.

Now, with the recent mandatory retirement of Judge Paul Harris Jr., we anticipate that the governor, with the stroke of a pen, will end this shameful lack of representation of people of color.

Women's History Month is an excellent opportunity to see how far we have come and how much further we need to go. This evening at 5, the Caucus of African-American Leaders will be celebrating Women's History Month. The meeting — at the Wiley H. Bates Legacy Center, 1101 Smithville St., Annapolis — will be open to the public. We will be joined by many candidates of both genders. A complimentary meal and beverage will be served.

The great feminist Coretta Scott King once said, "Women, if the soul of the nation is to be saved, I believe you must become its soul." This is precisely why I end this column with *A Luta Continua*, which means in Portuguese that the struggle continues for gender equality and peace.

Carl Snowden: Caucus of African American Leaders honors 'Her-Story'

March 11, 2019

Last year was called the Year of the Woman and indeed women won unprecedented seats nationally and locally.

Not since the elections of County Executive Janet S. Owens and Mayor Ellen O. Moyer have we seen women given power in an unprecedented manner.

As we celebrate Women's History Month, the Caucus of African-Americans Leaders is inaugurating a new award, the Her-Story Award, which will be given to women who have helped to break glass ceilings in politics and in the private sector.

Last month The Capital reported that women have been serving on the Annapolis City Council for 46 years. The city received its charter in 1708.

The first woman, the late Alderwoman Barbara Neustadt was not elected to the City Council until 1973 and Cynthia Abney Carter the first African-American woman was not elected until 1997. You do the math.

The late Anne Arundel County Councilwoman Sarah Carter was elected in 1974. She is the only African-American woman to serve on the County Council.

However, change is rapidly coming to Anne Arundel County with the election of State Senator Sarah Elfreth, Dels. Alice Cain, Sandy Bartlett, Heather Bagnall, Councilwoman Lisa Rodiven, Democratic Central Committee members Thea Boykins Wilson, Christine Davenport, Andrea Horton, School Board member Candace Antwine and Orphans Court Judge Vickie Gipson.

These are just a few of the women who are now elected officials. The history books will now have to record their individual achievements. These recent breakthroughs are a combination of hard work and an enlightened electorate.

As we see women candidates running for president of the United States, there are no longer the sexist barriers that existed when the late U.S. Rep. Shirley Chisholm sought the presidency in 1972.

At 5 p.m. Tuesday, the Caucus of African-American Leaders will be bestowing on scores of women the "Her-Story" awards.

Working with both County Executive Steuart Pittman and Mayor Gavin Buckley the caucus will be honoring legislators, entrepreneurs, activists, and mothers, who have made a difference in our community.

Whether it is Dee Goodwyn, a native Annapolitan that held a title of Vice President in a major corporation in the county, or filmmaker Vicky Bruce, whose groundbreaking film on the late Mayor Roger W. Moyer, Sr., and Joseph Zastrow Simms left indelible marks on the community.

The Her-Story reception is open to the public and will also feature a one-woman play performed by Scotti Preston. "Four Women" was written by local historian Janice Hayes Williams, now a member of Pittman's administration.

It was once observed that the talented Ginger Rogers could do something that Fred Astaire couldn't and that was dance backward while wearing high heel shoes.

Tuesday evening at the Wiley H. Bates Legacy Center, 1101 Smithville St. in Annapolis, the community is invited to join us for the Her-Story reception honoring all women for the contributions that they have made to our world.

My mom, who is 103-years-old, was born before women had the right to vote in America. On the eve of the centennial of women voting, we have witnessed first-hand the influence of women on our civil discourse.

It was the former First Lady Michelle Obama who said, when "they go low, we go high." The Her-Story awards given by the Caucus of African-American Leaders are about going high and making sure that all women are at the table of power and that they are both respected and protected by the electorate.

The reception is open to the public. Limited for the reception is on a first-come-first-served basis.

Until Her-Story is told, we will never have an accurate account of history. Her story is our story and the sooner we realize it, the better we will all be.

DR. MARTIN LUTHER KING, JR.

Carl O. Snowden

When I am asked, "What are your most proudest accomplishments?" I would say building monuments for Dr. Martin Luther King, Jr., Coretta Scott King and the Civil Rights Foot Soldiers Memorial. These monuments were built to remind future generations of the accomplishments and sacrifices that these individuals made.

I worked hand-in hand with the following people to successfully realize these achievements:

Shirley Alexander, Jacqueline Boone Allsup, Marc Apter, Theophilus Mahmoud Baptiste, Jeff Blum, Dr. Larry Blum, Morris H. Blum, Lewis Bracy, Gloria Butler, Gloria Criss, Christine Davenport, Lucille Davis, Mary Des Champs, Ann Dorsey, Robert Eades, Dr. Charlestine R. Fairley, Carol Gerson-Higgs, Dee Goodwyn, Joanna R. Hanes-Lahr, David J. Harris, Tina Marie Head, Frances Heath, Frederick Howard, Arlene Jackson, Jasper James, Lt. Clarence E. "Buckey" Johnson, Annapolis Police Chief Joseph S. Johnson, Daryl Jones, Esq., Michelle Le Furge, Alan Hilliard Legum, Erica Matthews, Bertina Nick, Wanda Soares Nottingham, Midgett S. Parker, Jr., Vaughn Phillips, Silas Price, Patrick Sarbeng, Dimitri Sfakiyanudis, J.T. "Kim" Sharps, Gail E. Smith, Anthony Smoot, Leslie Stanton, Tony Spencer, Mia Lissa Tompkins, Minister Tywana Tyler, LaVerne Walker, Ann Williams, John Wilson and Ann Marie Wood.

Over more than thirty years, these volunteers helped to raise money for three separate memorials: The Dr. Martin Luther King, Jr. Memorial, the only one in the State of Maryland, which is located at Anne Arundel Community College; the Coretta Scott King Memorial Garden located in Edgewater, Maryland: and the Civil Rights Foot Soldiers Memorial in the City of Annapolis. These memorials, all funded by private contributions were donated to educational and governmental entities.

We built them because we wanted future generations to know the impact that Dr. King had on each of us and the America he influenced and changed.

Carl Snowden: Remembering Dr. Martin Luther King Jr.

January 20, 2014

I was a teenager living in Annapolis when the Rev. Martin Luther King Jr. was assassinated in 1968. He was only 39, I was 14. Today, he would have been 85. It was one of the most traumatic experiences of my life.

Even today, having lived through the assassinations of Medgar Evers, President John F. Kennedy, Malcolm X and Sen. Bobby Kennedy, King's death still resonates with me.

I have lived long enough to see 10 presidents occupy the White House. I have lived through the Sept. 11, 2001 terror attacks and the Boston Marathon bombing. Indeed, I have been an eyewitness to some of America's greatest tragedies and triumphs.

I have become convinced the greatest honor we can pay King is to implement his social justice agenda and to remind future generations of the great sacrifices made to ensure every American would enjoy the privileges of citizenship in this nation.

Over the last decade, thanks to the generosity of ordinary citizens, we have built three memorials in Maryland. Each of these memorials was designed to educate a new generation about King and the foot soldiers who made it possible for us to enjoy the privileges we have today.

On the Arnold campus of Anne Arundel Community College, you will find the Martin Luther King Jr. Memorial. On the Edgewater campus of Sojourner Douglass College, you will find the Coretta Scott King Memorial Garden and in our state capital you will find the Civil Rights Foot Soldiers Memorial at Whitmore Park. These memorials were built as reminders of both how far we have come and how far we need to go.

In reading about and studying the life of King, I have come to appreciate his unselfish leadership. King understood leadership requires the ability to be resilient and to challenge the proposition that popularity is equivalent to justice. Prior to his assassination, King was not the beloved figure he has become.

The reality is that oftentimes one must be willing to challenge the status quo and suffer the consequences. King did both, and because he did our nation and world is a better place.

One of my favorite lines from a King speech is "having faith in the future." It is precisely that "faith" that I believe has made it possible to achieve the progress we have made. I often have said, "Some people watch clocks, I watch people and you can learn a great deal by watching them." I pay close attention to young people. Following is a poem for our youth:

Rosa sat;

Martin marched;

Malcolm warned;

Jesse ran;

Obama won;

Now what will you do?

Each generation has the responsibility and moral obligation to leave the world better than they inherited it. We can take great pride in our county in knowing we have more civil rights memorials per capita than any other jurisdiction in our state. Yet, the best way to truly honor King is to implement his social justice agenda.

Perhaps no public figure captured the spirit of this cause better than the late Senator Ted Kennedy, who said, "The work goes on, the cause endures, the hope still lives and the dream shall never die."

A Luta Continua, which means the struggle continues!

Carl Snowden: King's words as timely today as they were in the past

January 17, 2015

On January 15, 1955, a young man by the name of Martin Luther King, Jr. celebrated his 26th birthday. He had no way of knowing that 13 years later, he would become a martyr and change the course of history.

At the tender age of 26, he, as many black youth of his era, planned to live his life in a society that had predetermined what and who he may become.

At that time, he was not aware that a social movement was about to impact his life. He later referred to this movement as the "zeitgeist", defined as the trend or thought or feeling characteristic of a particular time period. He was on the eve of being involved in a whirlwind of social change. He had no way of knowing that he would never celebrate his 40th birthday.

In August, 1955, a black teenager by the name of Emmett Till visited Money, Mississippi. Shortly after his visit, he was murdered for allegedly whistling at a white woman. It was the brutal murder and mutilation of Emmett Till that so outraged blacks and would create the climate that produced what would later be called, "the modern civil rights movement."

In 1955, blacks were segregated in public accommodations. On December 1, 1955, a 42-year-old black woman, Rosa Parks, was arrested for refusing to give up her seat on a bus to a white man.

On December 5, 1955, King held a mass church rally, attended by thousands. During his speech, he said, "Sister Rosa, it is better that we walk in dignity than ride in shame." On that fateful day, the civil rights movement was launched.

For more than a year, blacks refused to use public transportation when it was blistering hot or bone chilling cold. Their determination was summed up by a woman named Mother Pollard who never attended college or a university but spoke for all when she said, "My feets are tired, but my soul is rested".

African-Americans were determined to change their social conditions at all cost. And what a cost it was. Thousands were jailed and hundreds lost their jobs and still others died on lonely highways. Eventually, the courts ruled that segregated bus accommodations were unconstitutional.

King would later be called the "Conscience of America." He was in the forefront of the greatest nonviolent social movement for justice that Americans had ever seen. During his 13 years of leadership, America was profoundly changed.

In 1964, he would meet Malcolm X. They were photographed together at the Capitol smiling. Martin and Malcolm would become two icons. Neither knowing that both history and fate would soon intervene and make them a symbolic pair forever.

One year after their meeting, Malcolm X was assassinated on February 21, 1965. Three years later, King would be assassinated on April 4, 1968. This year marks the 50th and 45th anniversaries of their respective assassinations. Those assassinations changed the course of history forever.

We will never know where this nation might have been had they lived. Neither would live long enough to be grandfathers, neither would see the fruits of their labor. Each would leave widows, orphan children and legacies that would endure decades after their deaths.

As we celebrate the birthday of King, let us remember what he said in the 20th century that rings true in the 21st century. We find ourselves still marching. Slogans like "We Shall Overcome" has been replaced by "We Can't Breathe."

The 20th century names of Emmett Till, Jimmie Lee Jackson, and Mack Parker have been replaced by the 21st century names of Michael Brown, Kendall Green, Eric Garner and Trayvon Martin.

This is why, King's words continue to resonate and inspire Americans. Words that are as timely today as they were yesterday; Words of hope and words of determination. Pause and you can hear the voice of King speaking to a new generation when he said,

"Our freedom was not won a century ago, it is not won today; but some small part of it is in our hands, and we are marching no longer by the ones and twos but in legions of thousands, convinced now it cannot be denied by any human force."

Information is power. Justice is indivisible. Truth is revealing and we must never abandon freedom. *A Luta Continua*, which means the struggle continues for justice and peace.

Carl Snowden: Annual dinner celebrates King's legacy

January 10, 2017

Friday is the official kickoff of a national celebration of the birthday of the Rev. Martin Luther King Jr. Hundreds are expected to attend the 29th Annual Dr. Martin Luther King Jr. Awards Dinner, the largest celebration of the Rev. King's birthday in Anne Arundel County. For nearly three decades, this dinner has attracted people from various racial, religious and political backgrounds.

This awards dinner, at 6 p.m. at La Fontaine Bleue in Glen Burnie, honors men and women who have demonstrated a propensity for justice. Over the years the dinner has raised more than $600,000 from the public to build memorials to educate future generations about the civil rights movement.

This Friday Anne Arundel County Police Chief Tim Altomare and Annapolis police Sgt. James C. Spearman Jr. will be honored for their leadership in addressing systemic racism in law enforcement. Both men have served the citizens of our county with integrity and taken seriously their oath "to serve and protect."

Others being honored include Alderman Kenneth A. Kirby and Dr. Alyson L. Hall, who will receive the first Alan Hilliard Legum Civil Rights Award, named after the late civil rights lawyer.

Dr. Hall and Alderman Kirby have supported the Dr. Martin Luther King, Jr. Committee in its efforts to create memorials in the county honoring the Rev. King, Coretta Scott King and the foot soldiers who made it possible for them and others to enjoy the privileges, they have today.

There are more civil rights memorials in this county than any in other jurisdiction in Maryland. These memorials were all paid for without tax dollars.

This year, Annapolis Fire Department Deputy Chief Kevin Simmons will receive the prestigious Morris H. Blum Award, named after the pioneering philanthropist who hired African-Americans as on-air personalities before the 1964 Civil Rights Act was enacted. This was unheard-of before 1964!

Other honorees include state Sen. Joan Carter Conway, Midshipman 1st Class Megan Rosenberger, Terry Patton, Alicia Smoot and Patience Schenck.

The theme of this year's dinner is "Out of a mountain of despair, a stone of hope." The theme is taking from the Rev. King's famous "I Have a Dream" speech.

This Friday we will be hearing from two major religious leaders. We are honored to have Bishop La Trelle Miller Easterling of the Baltimore-Washington Conference of the United Methodist Church, who will bring greetings.

Our dynamic keynote speaker will be the Rev. Kevin W. Cosby, president of Simmons College of Kentucky and the man who delivered the most passionate eulogy for the late Muhammad Ali. The Rev. Cosby captured the meaning and legacy of Ali, and we believe he will put in perspective the legacy of the Rev. King.

Also, attending the dinner will be U.S. Reps. John Sarbanes and C.A. Dutch Ruppersberger, County Councilman Pete Smith and former Annapolis police Chief Joseph S. Johnson.

More information on the dinner may be obtained by visiting the committee's website at www.mlkjr.md.org

What sets this dinner apart from others is that many of the patrons do not show up just once a year to honor the Rev. Martin Luther King Jr. but honor him daily by working to keep his dream alive.

The Caucus of African-American Leaders meets on the second Tuesday of each month at the Wiley H. Bates Legacy Center, 1101 Smithville St. in Annapolis. This meeting is open to the public as we continue to keep Dr. King's legacy alive.

Carl Snowden: Are we truly realizing King's dream?

December 20, 2017

The late Rev. Martin Luther King Jr. once said, "We are not makers of history. We are made by history."

This theme will be taken up at 9:30 a.m. on Jan. 6, at Room 219 in Anne Arundel Community College's Cade Center for Fine Arts. The Peer Learning Partnership, or PLP, an all-volunteer, self-governing community of lifelong learners that is part of the college's Center on Aging, will host a provocative symposium on race entitled: "Anne Arundel County: Are We Closer to the Dream? A Dialogue on Race." The partnership has asked me to keynote the event.

This symposium is free and open to the public and will kick off a series of events honoring the Rev. King's legacy.

There is a memorial statue on the AACC campus dedicated to the memory of the Rev. King, who was assassinated on April 4, 1968. It is the only statute in Maryland that specifically recognizes this Nobel Peace Prize winner. But the Civil Rights Foot Soldiers Memorial in Whitmore Park, across from the Arundel Center, has the Rev. King's image on it.

During the month-long celebrations of the Rev. King's birthday, there will be an awards dinner, a memorial breakfast, an event sponsored by the Office of the County Executive and a parade in Annapolis sponsored by the mayor's office.

But among these many activities in January, the PLP has decided that an honest dialogue on race is the best way to honor the Rev. King. How close in this county to fulfilling his dream of peace and brotherhood? Are we even willing to do so?

The PLP has assembled a distinguished panel to address these questions: noted historian and author Jane Wilson McWilliams; Charlestine R. Fairley, a retired educator; Thornell Jones, a community activist; and County Councilman Pete Smith. The event will be moderated by William Rowel.

James Dolan, one of the organizers, has indicated that this event, along with an additional series of events in February, will be an effort by the PLP to reach out to African-Americans, Latinos, Asians and others to make sure the dialogue continues.

As we begin to celebrate Kwanzaa and prepare for the New Year, I believe the Rev. King would be pleased to know that the PLP is celebrating his birthday by encouraging the entire community to take part in this epic dialogue.

Surely, he would be pleased to know that beyond memorials, breakfasts, dinners and parades, there are people dedicated to keeping his dream alive, through their words, deeds and actions.

Indeed, it was the moderator, Mr. Rowel, who once said that the "distance between dreams and reality is action." I salute the PLP for its action.

A Luta Continua, which in Portuguese means that the struggle continues!

Carl Snowden: Annual Dr. Martin Luther King Jr. dinner helps keep the dream alive

January 09, 2018

Friday marks two important milestones in my life. We will be celebrating the birthdays of Dr. Martin Luther King, Jr. and my mom, who will turn 102-years-old on that same day. What a blessing!

Dr. King, who was born on Jan. 15, 1929, would have been 89-years-old this month. He was assassinated on April 4, 1968.

This year marks the 30th year that we have paused to honor his legacy. We do this by honoring men and women who have kept his dream alive, through their words, deeds, and actions.

This year's honorees include Capt. Robert A. Dews Jr. of the Naval Academy; Delegate Joseline Pena Melnyk: retired Baltimore County Sgt. Randy Williams; a community activist Andre Atkins; Andre M. Mountain an educator; Janice Hayes Williams, a local historian; Earl "Tom" Schubert, a philanthropist and Kim J.T. Sharps, a member of the board of directors of the nonprofit Dr. Martin Luther King, Jr. Committee.

In addition, we will be honoring Philip Hunter, Esq., who, in 1965, was one of the brave Selma, Alabama marchers, who joined civil rights icon, U.S. Rep, John Lewis on what would later be called "Bloody Sunday", as they were beaten by Alabama State Troopers.

Also, we will be honoring the Rev. Stephen A. Tillett, president of the local NAACP and a member of the Caucus of African-American Leaders.

These individuals will be honored on Friday by U.S. Sen. Chris Van Hollen, U.S. Rep. C.A. Dutch Ruppersberger, U.S. Rep. John Sarbanes, U.S. Rep. Anthony Brown, Naval Academy Superintendent Vice Adm. Walter E. Carter, Jr., St. John's College President Panayiotis Kanelos, Annapolis Mayor Gavin Buckley, and first lady Julie Williams Buckley. Tickets will be sold at the door for this historic and gala event.

My mom, who was born in 1916, before women had the right to vote, has seen first-hand the difference that Dr. King made.

She lived in Annapolis when theatres, restaurants, bathrooms, housing, schools, employment and other public accommodations were segregated. She experienced Annapolis' apartheid on a daily basis.

On Friday and Saturday, God willing, she will see the Broadway Play, "I Have A Dream," being directed by Miami, Florida-based Herman Levern Jones of the Theatre South.

This play, which will be performed at the awards dinner and at 7 p.m. at St. John's College's Francis Scott Key Auditorium is a stark reminder that the struggle for peace and racial equality continues.

Here is what Dr. King said about the struggle for equality" "If you can't fly, then run, if you can't run, then walk, if you can't walk, then crawl, but whatever you do, keep moving forward."

This is why I end these columns with the Portuguese slogan, *A Luta Continua,* which means the struggle continues.

The Caucus of African-American Leaders meets on the second Tuesday of each month at the Wiley H. Bates Legacy Center, 1101 Smithville St. in Annapolis. This meeting is open to the public as we continue to keep Dr. King's legacy alive.

Happy birthday, mom, this column is dedicated to you.

Carl Snowden: Let's rename Whitmore Park to honor King

March 26, 2018

Just as I remember where I was when President John F. Kennedy was assassinated, I remember where I was when Dr. Martin Luther King Jr. was murdered on April 4, 1968.

A group of us teenagers were standing in front of the old Richmond Drug Store on the corner of West and West Washington streets when a young boy ran by us and shouted, "They killed Martin Luther King Jr."

We couldn't believe our ears. We rushed across the street, where a black-and-white television in a store's display window was showing images of Dr. King, but we could not hear the audio. A friend with a transistor radio tuned in to the WANN station, where we heard the station announcer say, "Dr. Martin Luther King Jr. was shot and killed in Memphis, Tennessee, this evening."

"Oh no," said one of the teenagers. Said another, "They have done it again." He kicked at the ground in anger.

A crowd formed of young black people from Clay, Larkin and Northwest and Washington streets. We were angry. No one said anything. Some of us started marching toward downtown. White merchants closed their stores. Black people were crying.

I will never forget the sense of hopelessness that day. That moment a half-century ago changed my life and the lives of my peers forever.

County Executive Steve Schuh and Mayor Gavin Buckley are scheduled to speak at noon on April 4 at the Civil Rights Foot Soldiers Memorial at Whitmore Park in Annapolis. There will be another observance at the same time located at the King memorial at Anne Arundel Community College. Both events are open to the public.

The Caucus of African-American Leaders has requested that government officials rename Whitmore Park the Martin Luther King Jr. Memorial Park. The nearby parking garage would continue to bear the name of John Whitmore, the first chairman of the Anne Arundel County Council under charter government.

Whitmore Park was where, 55 years ago, people boarded buses to attend the 1963 March on Washington during which Dr. King delivered his "I Have a Dream" speech. The park is in an area where, before the building of the Arundel Center and the Whitmore garage, there was a neighborhood with predominantly African-American residences and businesses.

Dr. King's last speech, "I Have Been to the Mountaintop" prophetically emphasized that we would have "some difficult days" ahead of us. Two months later, U.S. Sen. Robert F. Kennedy was assassinated in California.

Having lived through those tumultuous times, I know the role played by people like Mayor Roger W. Moyer Sr., Morris H. Blum, George Phelps Jr., Alderman Samuel Gilmer, the NAACP's Walter Blasingame, Marion Satterwaite, Marita Carroll, the Rev. Rufus Abernathy, Joseph "Zastrow" Simms and the Rev. Leroy Bowman, among others.

While over the years their roles have sometimes been exaggerated and embellished, they did offer hope and comfort. Mr. Blum allowed us to voice our views over WANN. The Rev. Bowman opened up First Baptist Church to young people and allowed all of us an opportunity to speak. Mayor Moyer walked the streets with Zastrow Simms and George Phelps, helping keep the community calm. Through tears and struggle, we were able to lift our spirits.

Some of us now plan to pay tribute to Dr. King by thanking God for his servant and keeping his struggle for social justice going. It would be a fitting and lasting tribute if county government officials were to name Whitmore Park in honor of Dr. King. If they do, I hope that they will have some of his timeless quotes throughout the park.

If you agree, call the Office of the County Executive at 410-222-1821 to express your support.

America lost a great voice 50 years ago. Now, it is up to us to remember him by implementing his unfinished agenda for peace and social justice. Every time you hear *A Luta Continua*, which means in Portuguese that the struggle continues, it is our way of honoring an apostle of peace who died valiantly for a cause greater than himself.

Carl Snowden: On the anniversary of King's speech, we must remember November

August 28, 2018

George Trotter and Kathleen Johnson have never met. They both live in Anne Arundel County.

One lives in Laurel and the other lives in Arnold. Both lives would be changed forever after hearing a preacher by the name of Martin Luther King, Jr. tells America about a dream he had. The year was 1963. The month was August. The numerical date was the 28th. The occasion was the 1963 March on Washington.

When they left their respective homes on that sweltering August day, neither knew that they had a date with destiny. Fifty-five years ago today, the civil rights movement in the 1960s would change America forever. Many reading this column will find it difficult to believe that an apartheid Anne Arundel County existed. African-Americans were denied employment opportunities, housing, and that racism was the order of the day.

Local Annapolis movie theatres like the Circle, Capitol and Playhouse didn't allow black people to patronize them. African-Americans were required to attend the Star theatre on Calvert Street.

Private clubs excluded people on the basis of their race and color. Local retail stores wouldn't allow black people to try on shoes, hats or clothing. If you lived in Anne Arundel County and you were an African-American, you were required to attend Wiley H. Bates High School, the only high school that blacks could attend under segregation.

I lived in Davidsonville and remember having to attend Carver Elementary School in Gambrills because we were not allowed to attend the white elementary schools. When my family moved to Annapolis, I saw first-hand signs that read "Colored" and "White." In downtown Annapolis, there once was a gas station that posted those demeaning signs. There were other signs too, signs that read, "No Jews, Negroes or dogs."

Kathleen Johnson was profiled in The Washington Post on the 50th anniversary of the march, she was quoted as saying, "When Dr. King was speaking, you could hear a pin drop." Today, the fifty-fifth anniversary of the March on Washington a lot has changed and yet there is so much more that needs to change.

Racism continues to play a pivotal role in the lives of many Americans. Whether it is African-Americans being arrested at a Starbucks or denied employment because they have "black sounding names", race continues to be a dominant factor in the body politic of America.

George Trotter was taken to Washington on that fateful day by the Rev. John T. Chambers Sr. I remember George, sharing with the audience on the 50th anniversary how he and Phil Chambers another participant felt that day, as he looked over an audience of thousands of people. He knew that this was watching history in the making.

Across from the Arundel Center is the Civil Rights Foot Soldiers Memorial, which has inscribed the names of many Anne Arundel County residents who attended that march 55 years ago today. Robert P. Duckworth, clerk of the court is listed as is the late Mayor Roger W. Moyer Sr., Morris H. Blum, Hannah Chambers, Judge Mary Sellman Jackson, Trudi McGowan, and literally hundreds or more.

When Martin Luther King Jr. delivered his "I Have A Dream" speech, sitting behind him was the Gospel singer Mahalia Jackson. As Dr. King began speaking, you can hear Mahalia Jackson shouting and exhorting him to, "tell them about the dream".

At one point, he left his written text and extemporaneously told America about his dream. This incredible speech is captured and is considered one of the greatest speeches ever delivered. On that day, he captured the hopes and dreams of millions of Americans.

In November, voters must remember that dreams like nightmares not only can happen while you are sleeping, they can also occur while you are voting. In November we must vote for our hopes and dreams, not the nightmare of going backward.

Carl Snowden: New class at Anne Arundel Community College will explore King's legacy

October 08, 2018

At 10 a.m. Oct. 20, Lester Brooks, PH.D. and I will co-teach a course HSY-381 entitled "The Life and Impact of Dr. Martin Luther King Jr." at Anne Arundel Community College. This course is a part of the community college's History and Heritage Fall series.

Brooks is a full-time professor in AACC's history department. He earned a bachelor degree from Indiana University, a master's degree from Howard University and a doctorate from the University of Michigan, all in the field of history. He has spent his entire life in academia.

I have spent my entire life as a civil rights activist. I worked as an adjunct professor at the community college and served as the first civil rights director for Maryland's Office of the Attorney General.

I served three terms on the Annapolis City Council and served in the cabinet of former county executive Janet S. Owens. I earned a Master of Human Services degree from Lincoln University in Pennsylvania and have lectured at various institutions of higher education around the nation.

What is often surprising is how much people do not know about King. People are astonished when I informed them that his mother was a victim of an assassin's bullet in 1974, just six years after his own assassination.

They are equally stunned to learn that she was murdered by an African-American.

I met King's father, the Rev. Martin Luther King Sr., when he came to Annapolis and delivered a sermon at Asbury United Methodist Church. "Daddy" King as he was affectionately called talked about his son and wife's assassination on that occasion.

I remember what happened in Annapolis following the murder of Dr. King. In an academic setting, we will share what King's impact had on each of us individually and on the world.

I was fortunate to have met the late Rosa Parks, who was arrested for not giving up her seat to a white man, during the era of segregation. Parks was part of a 381-day bus boycott in Montgomery, Alabama.

It was King who said during that boycott: "Sister Rosa, it is better that we walk in dignity rather than ride in shame."

The Caucus of African-American Leaders meets on the second Tuesday of each month at the Wiley H. Bates Legacy Center, 1101 Smithville St. in Annapolis. This meeting is open to the public as we continue to keep Dr. King's legacy alive.

Attendees will experience a lesson that King left his followers. At this meeting, attendees are asked to hold hands and tell people on their left and right that "I love you."

People are often uncomfortable when ask to do this exercise.

However, King knew that whenever Americans from various backgrounds join hands, we change the course of history.

In 1920, when we joined hands women won the right to vote. In 1965, when we joined hands the right to vote was guaranteed to African-Americans. In 1990, when we joined hands, we saw Nelson Mandela walked out a South African prison and into a presidency.

A Luta Continua is a Portuguese slogan that means that the struggle continues, for freedom, justice, peace, and love.

Carl Snowden: Looking back on 40 years of celebrating Dr. Martin Luther King Jr.'s legacy

January 07, 2019

In just 10 days we will pause to honor the memory and legacy of Martin Luther King, Jr. We have been celebrating the birthday of Dr. King in our county for almost 40 years.

I organized the first Dr. Martin Luther King Jr. Memorial Breakfast 38 years ago. I remember when the late Morris H. Blum, the Rev. Leroy Bowman, Bertina Nick, Lulu Hardesty, Alan Hilliard Legum, George Phelps Jr., Jerome "Skinny Butch" Simms and Delegate Aris T. Allen Sr. came to the first meeting. At that time King's birthday was neither a state nor national holiday.

Over the years, we marched, demonstrated and petitioned the government to make his birthday a holiday. In 1974, the late Delegate Kenneth L. Webster introduced the bill that made King's birthday a state holiday. I will always remember the late U.S. Rep. Parren J. Mitchell urging members of the General Assembly to vote for the bill.

Maryland became only the second state in the nation to make King's birthday a state holiday. The only Anne Arundel delegate to vote for the legislation was Allen. To their everlasting shame, no other member of the Anne Arundel County delegation voted for the bill.

We then joined with the late Coretta Scott King, Stevie Wonder, Dick Gregory and the Rev. Jesse Jackson to push for King's birthday to become a national holiday. After many marches, demonstrations and prayers President Ronald Reagan signed a bill in 1983 that made his birthday a national holiday.

By 1988, the Dr. Martin Luther King, Jr. Memorial Breakfast could no longer handle the crowd and we added the Dr. Martin Luther King, Jr. Awards Dinner. The dinner became the largest celebration of his birthday in the county.

Now, we have an annual Martin Luther King Jr. Parade, thanks in part to Priscilla Montague. Juanita Cage Lewis portrays Coretta Scott King in the parade and, of course, there are numerous church services held throughout the county in his memory.

Thanks to former County Executive Janet S. Owens, we have the only King memorial in Maryland located at Anne Arundel Community College.

King was one of those transforming figures whose impact on the world continues even after his death. Few public figures are able in death to evoke the emotional response that King has. I am so appreciative of this community, which has supported these events.

Beginning with a 5 p.m. reception at La Fontaine Bleue in Glen Burnie, we will honor 10 individuals who through their words, deeds and actions have kept alive King's dream.

The individuals who are being honored are George "Lassie" Belt, Patricia Cole, M. Eve Hurwitz, Wandra Ashley Williams, Vivian Gist Spencer, Najiba Hlemi, Midshipman First Class Aaron J. Lewis, Alderman Marc Rodriguez, U.S. Rep. C.A. Dutch Ruppersberger and U.S. Rep. John P. Sarbanes.

In addition, Alanna Dennis, Compliance Officer for the County will award Annapolis High School senior Zion Green with a King scholarship she is funding.

For more information regarding the Dr. Martin Luther King Jr. Dinner, visit www. mlkjrmd.org.

Tickets also can be purchased starting at 6 p.m. on Tuesday at the Caucus of African-American Leaders monthly meeting at the Wiley H. Bates Legacy Center, 1101 Smithville St., Annapolis. The caucus will hear from representatives from County Executive Steuart Pittman's Transition Team.

Whenever I think about King's dream, I think about the late U.S. Sen. Ted Kennedy who captured eloquently the spirit of that dream, when he said: "For me, a few hours ago, this campaign came to an end. For all those whose cares have been our concern, the work goes on, the cause endures, the hope still lives, and the dream shall never die."

A Luta Continua, which means in Portuguese, that the struggle continues and yes the dream shall never die.

Carl Snowden: How far have we come since King's assassination?

April 08, 2019

I was standing in front of the Richmond Drug Store on the corner of West and West Washington Street in Annapolis on April 4, 1968, when a black teenager shouted: "Martin Luther King, Jr. was shot."

On that infamous day, my life was changed forever. The gunshot that killed Dr. King also murdered something else on that day. America lost its innocence.

"We hold these truths to be self-evident..." took on a whole new meaning for my generation. In the more than a half-century since the death of King, I have seen and witnessed more violence than I thought would have been possible.

I was part of a generation that marched for peace in Vietnam and justice at home. My generation saw the assassinations of Medgar Evers, President John F. Kennedy, Malcolm X, Dr. King, and Sen. Robert F. Kennedy.

Last week, I attended two roundtable discussions. Each of them was poignant reminders on how far we have come and must go.

The first roundtable forum was held at the Anne Arundel Medical Center on the subject of gun violence and was organized by U.S. Rep. John Sarbanes. The hour-long discussion focused on the mass shootings that have occurred all over the nation.

The journalists murdered at The Capital last year, Jews murdered at a Pittsburgh synagogue, African-American churchgoers murdered in South Carolina and students of every age and hue killed at far too many schools to list.

I listened intently to County Executive Steuart Pittman and Mayor Gavin Buckley as they discussed what local government can do about the problem of violence.

Retired Annapolis police Sgt. James Spearman shared with us his more than three decades of experience and discussed what he believed was needed to address the problem.

His comments like those of local NAACP President Jacqueline Allsup echoed King's vision of a society that simply treated all of its people fairly.

How much better would we have been if we had taken King's philosophy of nonviolence more seriously?

The second roundtable discussion I attended was organized by the quasi-governmental entity Arundel Community Development Services and focused on the impediments to fair housing in the county.

One of those impediments is that the county, unlike other counties, does not have a fair housing law and its Human Relations Commission has no subpoena power.

The disparities in homeownership by race and ethnicity in the county is alarming. White homeowners make up 80% of the county population, black homeowners are just 51% and Latinos 56%. In the City of Annapolis, only 38% of African-Americans are homeowners.

This data and other recent events suggest now is the time to look at how far, we have come as a city and county in achieving the beloved community that King gave his life for.

The Caucus of African-American Leaders meets on the second Tuesday of each month at the Wiley H. Bates Legacy Center, 1101 Smithville St. in Annapolis. This meeting is open to the public as we continue to keep Dr. King's legacy alive. We have invited and they have accepted County Executive Pittman, Capital Gazette Editor Rick Hutzell and WNAV News Director Jane Schleger to be on a panel that looks at how we can implement King's vision of the beloved community.

The forum, open to the public will take place at the Wiley H. Bates Legacy Center, 1101 Smithville St. in Annapolis. The event is open to the public and a complimentary dinner will be served.

We elect people to solve problems. Now, is the time to honor the memory of King by solving problems. His powerful words, "It's either nonviolence or nonexistence" still resonate.

A Luta Continua, which is Portuguese and means that the struggle continues for peace, equality and justice.

HISTORY & MALCOLM X

Carl O. Snowden

I love history and I believe in learning the lessons of historical matters. Decisions I make are often grounded in history. It is so important that people take the time to study and learn from the past. I grew up in Annapolis, a city that prides itself on its own history.

Annapolis was once the capital of the United States of America. The city was incorporated in 1708 and became the temporary capital of the U.S. after the signing of the Treaty of Paris in 1783.

It is where George Washington resigned from the Continental Congress on December 23, 1783 as the Commander in Chief of the Continental Army. Two signers of the Declaration of Independence were Annapolitans: Charles Carroll and William Paca. Also, Annapolis is the home of the United States Naval Academy.

It's State House once housed an infamous statue to Chief Judge Roger Taney, who authored that awful Dred Scot Decision, which said in essence that blacks had no rights that whites are bound to respect.

However, too often its history was not all-inclusive and generally left out people of color. Annapolis has a rich history as it relates to Black people. It is a history that dichotomy is based on American styled apartheid. Nonetheless, it is not unlike other cities and states in America.

In Annapolis, we had the dubious distinction of having the lynching of a black man named Henry Davis near St. John's College. There was also the 1919 execution by hanging of a black man named John Snowden (no relation) who received a posthumous pardon 80 years later by then Governor Parris Glendenning.

Our city elected William Butler as the first black public official in the State of Maryland in 1873 as an alderman of the city of Annapolis.

However, it took 367 years before a governor in our state appointed a woman of color to the Anne Arundel County Circuit Court. Her name is Elizabeth Morris. To This day, no Latino, Asian or Native American has ever served on the aforementioned court and only three black men have ever served on this Judicial body.

Kunte Knite was brought from Africa in 1767 and sold into slavery in Annapolis, Maryland. I would later meet and interview the late Alex Haley, his famous descendant who collaborated with Malcolm X on his autobiography.

This is the reason why I wanted us to build a memorial in Annapolis to Kunte Kinte in 1978.

My admiration to Malcolm X is so great that I named both of my sons in honor of him and have the only plaque dedicated to his memory in front of my home.

Not only were people of color excluded from Annapolis' history, but so were woman. In a subsequent chapter, my views on this subject will be self-evident.

Carl Snowden: Remembering a historic decision

Carl O. Snowden and schoolmates leaving school

May 17, 2014

Sixty years ago today, the U.S. Supreme Court handed down its famous Brown v. Board of Education decision. This momentous decision called for the desegregation of all public schools "with all deliberate" speed.

In order to put this landmark decision into historical context, here in Anne Arundel County, the only high school African-Americans could attend was the old Wiley H. Bates High School in Annapolis.

No matter where you lived in Anne Arundel County, if you were black, you were required to attend this high school. If you lived in Glen Burnie, Shady Side, Laurel, Arnold, Severna Park, Deale, Brooklyn or Maryland City, you were required to go to Wiley H. Bates High School.

In fact, every native African-American has a member of their family who once attended this once-segregated school. It was not unusual for elders to tell their children, "Boy, get a good education, it is the one thing that they cannot take from you."

Parents and grandparents who had experienced the horrors and realities of racism in its rawest forms would say to the youth of my generation, "You have to be twice as smart to get half as far."

Now, six decades later, there is no question the political landscape of America has changed. When the 1954 decision was handed down, there were no women, Latinos or African-Americans on the Supreme Court. The most prominent African-American in 1954, was New York Congressman Adam Clayton Powell Jr.

The world had not heard of Rosa Parks, Malcolm X or the Rev. Martin Luther King Jr. and the NAACP was considered a "radical" organization.

Here is Anne Arundel County, all of the movie theaters were segregated. The Playhouse on Main Street, the Circle Theatre on Church Circle, The Star Theatre on Calvert Street and the Capitol Theatre on West Street were all segregated, as were the restaurants, bars, taverns and department stores.

Annapolis would not have its first sworn African-American police officers until 1960 and African-Americans in Annapolis were concentrated in the old Ward 4, or the" black belt," as it was affectionately called.

For nonnative residents, the Ward 4 streets included Larkin, Pleasant, Clay, West Washington, Calvert, Northwest and other streets comprising a then thriving African-American community also known as "Uptown."

During this era, I lived in "downtown" Annapolis, which, believe it or not, once was populated by African-Americans. I lived on Fleet and Cornhill Streets. I used to get my hair cut at Roger Williams' Barbershop.

When the Supreme Court handed down its decision, it would change America forever. As a little boy, I remember the "White" and "Colored" signs at the old gas station at the foot of Main Street. I remember when the Ku Klux Klan held a demonstration at the State House.

I remember being bused from my grandfather's home in Davidsonville past the elementary school closest to my home to attend the then segregated George Washington Carver Elementary School in Gambrills.

On this anniversary, it is important to pause, reflect, mediate, pray and to thank God and his servants for helping to change the apartheid America that once existed legally in our nation.

I want to take a moment to thank the late educator, Walter S. Mills, whom Parole Elementary School is named after. He, along with the late NAACP lawyer and future Associate Justice Thurgood Marshall, made it possible for equal pay for black and white teachers in Anne Arundel County. This case would serve as an underpinning for the Brown decision.

Also, I want to thank the grandmothers, grandfathers and parents of that era, who, through sheer determination, made it possible for our children and grandchildren to have opportunities that were denied to them solely based on the color of their skin.

It was those people who huddled in their churches every Sunday and prayed to God that one day their children's children would have opportunities that were denied them.

Now, 60 years later, many of us understand what they meant when they admonished us and said, "You have to be twice as smart to get half as far."

We are not quite there yet, but thanks be to God and a determined people, we are closer than we have ever been.

A Luta Continua. The struggle continues.

Carl Snowden: Bond, Israel both men of principle

August 25, 2015

The late NAACP emeritus Chairman Julian Bond and Alderman Richard Israel were two kindred souls. Each left an indelible mark, respectively on the nation and in their community. I was fortunate to know them both.

Julian Bond was a founding member of the Student Nonviolent Coordinating Committee and an associate of the Rev. Martin Luther King Jr. He recently died at age 75.

Bond was elected to the Georgia House of Representatives and was denied admittance in 1965 because of his anti-Vietnam War stance. He was seated in 1967 after the U.S. Supreme Court ruled unanimously that he had to be admitted.

He became a national figure when he was nominated in 1968 to be vice president of the United States at the National Democratic Convention, a nomination he had to turn down because, at 28, he was too young to hold that office. Eventually, in 2008, he would become a friend and confidant of President Barack Obama, the first African-American president of the United States.

In 1996, Bond spoke at an annual Dr. Martin Luther King Jr. Awards Dinner in Anne Arundel County. He was introduced by Vincent O. Leggett, who told the audience, "This is Julian Bond, not James Bond." Bond smiled and said, "We both made our mark."

Julian Bond became one of the first major civil rights figures to support gay rights, including marriage equality. He believed no one should be discriminated against based on their sexual orientation, race, nationality, gender or religion.

He would have liked the late Alderman Richard Israel. Israel, who died at the age of 72, also made history.

I remember when Israel, who was a lawyer and had served as an assistant state attorney general, was chairman of the Annapolis Board of Supervisors of Elections. In 1997, Cynthia Abney Carter was elected as the first African-American woman on the Annapolis City Council. She had run as a write-in candidate and her election was decided by the Board of Elections.

Israel, along with Gertrude "Trudi" McGowan, cast the decisive, historic votes that allowed Carter to become an alderwoman.

Israel said at the time that he was proud to have cast that vote, a vote, he said was based on law and principle. Indeed, when he was elected an alderman in his own right he demonstrated over and over again that he was a man of principle. He worked with local historian Janice Hayes-Williams to ensure that Maryland's role in the Civil War was recognized and celebrated.

One of my fondest memories of Dick Israel dates from 2005, the 40th anniversary of the historic 1965 Voting Rights Act, when as a commemoration of that historic act we had decided to run African-American candidates in every ward. Unlike other council incumbents, Israel not only embraced the idea but personally picked up his opponent, who lived in the Bloomsbury Square public housing community and took her to every candidate debate and forum.

He not only won the election, he also won the admiration of an entire community.

Before his health deteriorated, Israel attended the annual Dr. Martin Luther King Jr. Awards Dinner. At the 1996 dinner at which Julian Bond spoke, Dick Israel was there nodding in agreement with Bond's assertions that America was moving in the right direction and that there was more work to be done in festinating (hurrying) our nation to live up to its principles.

At 3:30 p.m. Sept. 1, there will be a memorial service for Alderman Israel at St. Anne's Episcopal Church in Annapolis. It will be an opportunity for citizens to pay their respects to him. I plan on attending and taking my grandchildren.

Israel and Bond, were two men of the same generation who shared a similar principle and came to the same conclusion: What makes America great is when all Americans' rights are respected and protected. I suspect that when the bells in heaven ring, Julian and Dick will be joining hands and saying "I'm glad to meet a kindred spirit."

A Luta Continua, which in Portuguese means, "The struggle continues!"

Carl Snowden: Mitchell's life's work to be honored

September 03, 2015

On this Friday at 7 p.m. the West County Democratic Club will be inauguratng its first Congressman Parren J. Mitchell Awards Dinner. The keynote speaker will be civil rights attorney Barbara Arwine. The dinner will be held at Club Meade, 6600 Mapes Road, Building 6600, Fort George G. Meade.

Former Councilman Daryl Jones, the first African-American male elected to the Anne Arundel County Council, wanted to honor a man who had contributed so much to our state and nation. And I must say it is long overdue. Mitchell was the first African-American elected to the House of Representatives from Maryland. He had the oratorical skills of Martin Luther King Jr. and the charisma of Malcolm X. He was one of the founding members of the Congressional Black Caucus.

His courage and his audacity made him one of the most outstanding congressmen of all time.

First elected to the House in 1971, he retired from Congress in 1987. When asked why he was retiring from a "safe" seat, Mitchell responded, "Always leave when people are shouting 'encore — and never look back."

Mitchell opened doors that had been closed to people of color. He served in the U.S. Army during World War II and he was the first black to attend graduate school at the University of Maryland, College Park, after winning a lawsuit against the university to make it admit African-Americans. Daryl Jones credits Mitchell with getting him the opportunity to become a lawyer.

I had the pleasure of interviewing Mitchell when I hosted the "Community Viewpoint" radio program on WANN radio in Annapolis. During one of those interviews, he talked about meeting whites who did not want to acknowledge that racism existed. They were either "dumbfounded or were founded dumb," he said.

Although he was elected from the 7th Congressional District of Baltimore City, he frequently was the only black congressman in Maryland at the time and many African-Americans viewed him as "our" congressman. We called on him numerous times to assist us in Annapolis regarding affordable housing, racism and disparity in education. He always answered our call.

Mitchell's life was threatened by the Ku Klux Klan and white supremacists, and he received few accolades from conservatives. He ran for lieutenant governor on a ticket with former state Attorney General Stephen A. Sachs. At my home, I have a photo of myself standing with Mitchell behind the late Gov. Marvin Mandel, who had just signed the bill to make Martin Luther King Jr.'s birthday a state holiday.

Mitchell encouraged and endorsed me when I ran for alderman and won my first term on the Annapolis City Council and supported me in every subsequent election I ran.

Two of the saddest moments in my life involved Mitchell. When he died at age 85 in 2007, I mourned, knowing we would never see another like him in my lifetime. And a few years ago, when I was asked to speak at a Black History Month event, not a single student in a history class knew who he was. I cried.

I did not and cannot blame them, however. I blame our leadership for failing to preserve Mitchell's place in history.

I have never understood why the African-Americans who followed Mitchell to Congress never spearheaded a fundraising campaign to build a memorial to him. Every child should know that George Washington was our nation's first president and every child in Maryland should also know that our first black congressman was Parren J. Mitchell.

I thank the West County Democratic Club for inaugurating this dinner. It is my hope and prayer that someone in Maryland will spearhead an effort to honor a man who never said "no" to any cause that advanced humanity. The least we can do is to honor his memory by insisting that our children know who he was.

I thank the West County Democratic Club for honoring my hero. *A Luta Continua*, which, in Portuguese, means that the struggle continues.

Carl Snowden: NAACP's struggle still crucial

November 10, 2015

The National Association for the Advancement of Colored People is the oldest and largest civil rights organization in America. It was founded in 1909 and its mission was to eradicate racial discrimination. The Anne Arundel County branch was founded in 1944, with the same mission focused on Anne Arundel County.

Former presidents have included the late Constance Y. Brown, the Rev. John T. Chambers Sr., Alderman Samuel Gilmer, Lulu Hardesty, the Rev. David H. Croll, Dr. Theodore Johnson and the Rev. Leon H. White. Croll and Medgar Evers are the only NAACP leaders to have streets named after them in Annapolis: Croll Drive and Medgar Evers Street.

More recent NAACP presidents have been Dr. Jean Creek, Gerald Stansbury, Alva Sheppard Johnson and Jacqueline Boone Allsup. The current president is the Rev. Stephen A. Tillett.

Full disclosure: I am a proud life member of the NAACP and have served in its state and local branches.

NAACP membership at the national level reads like who's who of American history: President Barack Obama, Supreme Court Associate Justice Thurgood Marshall, U.S. Rep. Parren J. Mitchell, U.S. Sen. Edward Brooke, Rosa Parks, the Rev. Martin Luther King Jr., Dorothy Height, Angela Davis, James Baldwin and Maya Angelou.

In Anne Arundel County, members have included William F. Chaney, Morris H. Blum, Hannah Chambers, former Annapolis police Chief Joseph S. Johnson, Walter Blasingame, former schools Superintendent Kevin Maxwell, Daryl Jones, Dee Goodwyn, the Rev. Leroy Bowman and George Phelps Jr.

The NAACP remains one of the nation's most important civil rights organizations. Its illustrious history is replete with legal victories, including a 1915 U.S. Supreme Court decision that restored the voting rights of African-Americans in Annapolis.

The organization led the battle to get equal pay for African-American educators in the county. Thanks to the late Walter S. Mills and Thurgood Marshall, that decision paved the way for the famous Brown vs. Board of Education of Topeka Supreme Court case that led to the desegregation of public schools in America.

In more recent times, it was the NAACP and the American Civil Liberties Union (to which I also belong) that struck down an unconstitutional anti-loitering law passed by the Annapolis City Council.

The NAACP filed successful voting rights cases, which led to greater political representation. It also joined with other community groups in filing a complaint against the Anne Arundel County Public Schools that resulted in the Board of Education agreeing to eliminate the achievement gap.

Several weeks ago, the NAACP joined with the Caucus of African American Leaders to host a town hall meeting on systemic racism in our county.

The NAACP remains in the vanguard of the social justice movement. It was the NAACP, under the leadership of Gerald Stansbury, that supported the Dream Act and marriage equality legislation, both passed by the General Assembly.

The local branch of the NAACP will hold its 41st annual Freedom Fund Awards Banquet starting 7 p.m. Friday at the DoubleTree by Hilton Hotel in Annapolis. This event will once again allow the community to thank volunteers, who have paved the way for the progress we have enjoyed at the local level.

Also, it will allow readers to join a venerable organization that, since its founding, has understood what the late abolitionist Frederick Douglass understood: Where there is struggle, there is progress. As Douglas stated "if there is no struggle, there is no progress."

It was the great Frederick Douglass who also said, "It is not the light that we need, but fire; it is not the gentle shower, but thunder. We need the storm, the whirlwinds and the earthquake."

Also, I might add, that we need the NAACP, for, as is embodied in its mission, we need to eradicate racism, which is precisely why the Portuguese saying, *A Luta Continua*, is so appropriate. It means, "the struggle continues!"

Carl Snowden: Social divides are real, but can be bridged

April 12, 2016

The African-American educator Philip L. Brown wrote a book called "The Other Annapolis." Mr. Brown, who died at age 100, has a building in downtown Annapolis named after him and his wife Rachel Hall Brown, thanks to former school board President Vincent O. Leggett, Mr. and Mrs. Brown's son Erroll Sr., other community activists and the Anne Arundel County School Board.

These educators impacted the lives of many people and are fondly remembered. But I'm sure thousands of pedestrians and motorists passing that building on Green Street do not know who the Browns were — just as I'm many are unaware the Johnson Building at Anne Arundel Community College is named after the African-American educator Catherine Johnson.

The "other" Annapolis is often stereotyped and underrepresented in the governance of our city, county and state.

Do we measure social progress by the number of people represented by our legislative bodies? By the number of minority-owned and minority-operated businesses? By our various houses of worship?

The Rev. Martin Luther King Jr. once observed that 11 a.m. — the time of Sunday services — is the most segregated hour in America. He knew why there were separate places of worship, just as we know why there are "black" and "white" cemeteries.

Literally hundreds, if not thousands, of people have never visited the "other" Annapolis. They have no idea where the Eastport Colored School once stood on Chester Avenue or why blacks were excluded from private clubs and jobs in local and state government.

Every time this subject is raised, people are immediately accused of playing "the race card." In fact they are talking about their own history, and it's important that history not be forgotten. It's equally important that lessons are learned — so that history is not repeated.

I am a graduate of the Key School, a predominantly white, upper middle-income school. I became familiar with Annapolitans who never visited a public housing community or set foot in an African-American church.

Attending Key School greatly enriched my life, affording me opportunities not available to many of my peers. And I learned the difference between opportunity and wealth.

I did not pass French and needed to take summer school. A white schoolmate was in the same situation. That summer I went to St. John's College and was tutored by a French teacher for six weeks, while my schoolmate was sent to Paris — because her parents had been told students immersed in the culture could master the language in no time.

We both passed French that year. I remember my classmate telling me what it was like to be in Paris for six weeks at age 16. And her experience gave me a glimpse of an Annapolis I did not know. I learned to say "pass the margarine" in French; she learned to say "pass the butter" in French.

I soon realized that there was an "other Annapolis" beyond public housing — places like the Naval Academy, the State House and City Hall. Places with symphonies, plays and musicals.

I have met native Annapolitans who have never been in the State House or the Naval Academy. I know people who have never sailed or been asked to attend a symphony orchestra concert. My experiences allowed me to see both sides of the other Annapolis Mr. Brown wrote about.

A monthly meeting was held at the Wiley H. Bates Legacy Center, 1101 Smithville St. in Annapolis, where the Caucus of African-American Leaders brought together whites, blacks, Latinos and others to discuss issues impacting this county. The meeting was open to the public.

Candidates will be there seeking votes. For some, I suspect, it will be their first meeting with people from the other Annapolis Philip Brown documented.

There is a huge portrait of Philip Brown in the meeting room. I am sure that from the heavens above Mr. Brown will be saying *A Luta Continua*, which in Portuguese means "the struggle continues!"

Carl Snowden: Remembering President Kennedy's assassination

November 22, 2016

The year was 1963. It started off as just another beautiful day. I was in class at Annapolis Elementary School on Green Street. Suddenly, my homeroom teacher came into our classroom. She was crying. She told us that we were dismissed and could go home early.

We shouted in joy and in unison. It was a Friday and we were getting out of school early.

I lived in downtown Annapolis at the time. I was a walker. As I joined with my friends in taking the short walk from Green Street to Pinkney Street, I noticed that all of the adults were either crying or agitated. I had no idea why.

When I reached my home, my family had surrounded a small black-and-white television set. Some of them were crying. As I looked at the television screen, I saw a reporter, who said, "President Kennedy has been shot."

Some people in my family pontificated that this happned because President John F. Kennedy was trying to help African-Americans. Others thought he was killed because of his ideology.

Even though, I was just a youngster, I instinctively knew that something serious had taken place. The assassination of President Kennedy was my first recognition that America had lost its innocence.

It has been 53 years since Kennedy's tragic assassination, yet, for my generation this milestone will never be forgotten.

I have been an eyewitness to history. I have seen bullets and not ballots change the course of history.

I lived through the assassinations of President Kennedy, Malcolm X, Martin Luther King Jr. and Sen. Robert F. Kennedy, all in one decade. The places in Dallas, Harlem, Memphis and Los Angeles where each of these men were gunned down are stark reminders of what a bullet can do and how dreams can be shattered.

How different America might have been had any of these leaders lived longer. President Kennedy's call to action — when he said, "My fellow Americans, ask not what your country can do for you, ask what you can do for your country" – inspired a whole generation, including me.

I saw firsthand that people responded to his call of service. Students marched for peace and civil rights. Leaders advocated racial equality. Environmentalists worked to preserve the Earth. There was a sense that we were part of a great movement for social change.

Then the unthinkable happened — one assassination after another.

I wept when Malcolm was murdered. I prayed when Martin Luther King Jr. was gunned down. And after the assassination of Bobby Kennedy, it took me a long time to believe that change could come from ballots and not bullets.

On this 53rd anniversary of President Kennedy's assassination and looking ahead to the inauguration of a president-elect who became more famous for advocating building walls than building bridges, my faith is unshaken. I have faith in the future.

I know that there is a power in the universe that put wetness in water and blue in the sky, and that allows birds to fly. I know that history is replete with examples of progress being made against great obstacles. I know that every knock-down is not a knockout.

Every now and then, it is important to reflect on the words of President Kennedy when he said, "Mankind must put an end to war or war will put an end to mankind." It was the Rev. King who said, "Only when it gets dark enough can you see the stars."

I believe that our best days are ahead of us. In the words of Frederick Douglass, "Where there is progress, there is struggle."

On the anniversary of President Kennedy's assassination, it is in that spirit that I say *A Luta Continua*, which in Portuguese means the struggle continues.

Carl Snowden: An 'apology' doesn't go far enough

February 14, 2017

On Monday, descendants of the only Marylander to serve as chief justice of the U.S. Supreme Court plan to go to the statue of Roger B. Taney in front of the State House to issue an "apology" for the court's infamous decision in Dred Scott v. Sanford, issued on March 6, 1857.

The 7-2 decision said, in effect, that black people had no rights white people were bound to respect. The Supreme Court 7-2 decision said Dred Scott, a slave who had been taken to free territory, could not sue in federal court to escape servitude. It was the most racist decision the Supreme Court ever handed down, affirming for white supremacists their belief that white people were superior to blacks — a lie that, 160 years later, reminds us how deeply rooted racism was in this nation by law, custom and practice.

A guest column in The Capital a few years ago by Anne Arundel County Circuit Court Judge Paul G. Goetzke defended Taney, saying in essence that he was a "man of his times" and should be judged that way. It's the same logic some apply to slaveholding Founding Fathers. We are told Thomas Jefferson, who wrote the magnificent words, "We hold these truths to be self-evident, that all men are created equal" should be given a pass on the fact he owned slaves.

Soon after the Civil War, the state commissioned the statue of Taney on the State House grounds. Thousands of tourists pass it every year, most with no idea of who Taney was or why he occupies such a prominent location.

Twenty years ago, civil rights advocates pressured the state into erecting a statue of Thurgood Marshall, the Marylander who was the first African-American justice on the Supreme Court, on Lawyers Mall. Some say this "balances" Taney's statue. I respectfully disagree.

Taney's descendants are to be joined on Monday, as a gesture of support, by William Haley, the son of Alex Haley, and other descendants of Kunta Kinte, brought to Annapolis in chains in 1767. But reconciliation, unless it is accompanied by reparations, is a hollow gesture.

How does an "apology" address slavery, the Middle Passage, the Jim Crow laws, the lynchings, the institutional racism and the dreadful Dred Scott decision, which led to so many atrocities during the more than a century of oppression, exploitation and degradation it sanctioned.

The men who wore black robes in 1857 were in sync with the men who later wore white robes and terrorized black people. These terrorists and night riders agreed with the reasoning of the Dred Scott decision.

I have no doubt of the sincerity of the well-meaning people organizing Monday's apology. But for this gesture to mean anything, it must be accompanied by action that seeks to remedy the situation.

There is ample precedent. In 1988, Congress gave reparations to Japanese-Americans whose families were interned during World War II. Congress entered into treaties with Native Americans to compensate them for land that was confiscated. In 1953, West Germany and Israel entered into the Luxembourg Agreement, resulting in reparations for Jewish victims of the Holocaust.

There has been nothing equivalent for African-Americans. In the final days of the Civil War, on Jan. 16, 1865, Union Gen. William T. Sherman, trying to go beyond Lincoln's Emancipation Proclamation in addressing the wrongs of slavery, promised formerly enslaved African-American farmers 40 acres and a mule — something that never happened.

I commend the organizers of Monday's event. But if justice means anything, it must mean more than a symbolic gesture — it must be accompanied by real reform. The organizers should seriously consider asking the state to follow their apology with action resulting in reparations. You can bet that this would put Maryland in the vanguard of real change.

I wish the organizers luck, but I think they will discover that issuing an apology, by itself, will neither change history nor make amends for America's greatest sin.

A Luta Continua, which means in Portuguese that the struggle continues!

Carl Snowden: Courage more important than color

March 27, 2017

I have always admired courageous people. Many of them have shaped my views about everything from being a parent to taking on what, sometimes, appears to be the impossible.

People who read my columns know of my great admiration for the Dr. Martin Luther King Jr., Malcolm X and Rosa Parks. What may surprise some is my appreciation, love and respect for white people I have known over the years who have stood up and spoken out when so many others were silent.

One was Morris H. Blum, who in 1947 founded WANN radio. Years before the 1964 Civil Rights Act mandated equal opportunity, he hired African-Americans, including Charles "Hoppy" Adams Jr., who was the first black on-air personality. I got to know Mr. Blum very well over the years and will always remember his stories about Annapolis in the 1940s and 1950s.

C. Christopher Brown and the late Alan H. Legum and were two lawyers who did what many in their profession do not do — they took principled stands.

Brown used his skills to have the representation of African-Americans increased on the City Council. His recent book, "The Road to Jim Crow," is an eye-opening account of the statewide impact of the struggle of African-Americans on the Eastern Shore.

The legacy of Brown and Legum is reflected in the composition of our local government, as their lawsuits opened up opportunities that women and African-Americans have taken advantage of and that have subsequently affected the makeup of our police and fire departments.

When I was a teenager, Marion Satterwaite often took groups of us to get people registered to vote. She sometimes made her neighbors and others angry, but she was always there, as were Carol Gerson Higgs and Susan Goering.

Then there were Mayor Roger W. "Pip" Moyer Sr., County Executive Janet S. Owens, U.S. Rep. Marjorie S. Holt and Anne Arundel County Circuit Court Judge Warren B. Duckett Jr., who often took controversial stands in defense of civil rights and civil liberties.

When I was on the City Council, I introduced legislation that prohibited private clubs in Annapolis from discriminating based on race and gender, and venomous and vile opposition manifested itself in ugly letters and racist comments. That bill passed by just one vote, and I will always remember Alderwoman Ruth Gray voting for that ordinance despite the vocal and nasty opposition, she received.

I graduated from the Key School because of Headmaster Ted Oviatt and a group of white people who paid for my tuition after I was expelled from Annapolis High School for leading a demonstration against the school system.

Experience has taught me that people are complex and often contradictory. When you take an unpopular stand, you will find out who your true friends are — and will know them not by their color but by the courage they show.

In truth, bigots and racists don't frighten me. I have seen how their comments are often masked in anonymity and cowardice. I have had the dubious distinction of having the Ku Klux

Klan march in front of City Hall denouncing me, and of receiving death threats from the darker quarters of some sick minds.

The Rev. Martin Luther King Jr. once said. "There comes a time when one must take a position that is neither safe, nor politic, nor popular, but he must take it because conscience tells him it is right." I am delighted to have lived during an era when I have seen people of all colors, religions, genders and nationalities stand up for what they believe is right.

I have learned in life that courage and fear cannot occupy the same space at the same time. Those who will stand with you and who do it at great peril are not only courageous, but they are the best friends you will ever have.

I have known such people and I am eternally indebted to them. This is why I am able to continue to say *A Luta Continua*, which in Portuguese means that the struggle continues — and it a struggle that is based on one's courage, not one's color.

Carl Snowden: Schuh understands the importance of transparency

July 24, 2017

Today, members of the Caucus of African-American Leaders are meeting with County Executive Steve Schuh at the Arundel Center. These quarterly meetings are held to discuss a variety of issues.

The caucus has had U.S. Sens. Chris Van Hollen and Ben Cardin; U.S. Reps. John Sarbanes and Anthony Brown; House of Delegates Speaker Michael E. Busch; County Councilmen Pete Smith, Chris Trumbauer and Andrew Pruski; Alderman Kenny Kirby and a host of other elected officials speak to its membership. These meetings are informative and often action-oriented.

More importantly, they keep the lines of communications open. The discussions are always frank and respectful. We have discovered that there are areas we can agree upon. One of them is transparency.

That is why our meetings with the county executive have proven so productive. Mr. Schuh knows there is a lack of trust in government today. He knows that one of the ways to restore this is through transparency.

His administration agreed to post incidents involving discriminatory complaints online. Now, with a click of a mouse, citizens can find out what county departments have received complaints and what the disposition of those complaints have been.

Mr. Schuh agreed to hire a compliance officer. We're expect an update today on the status of that hiring.

One of Mr. Schuh's early appointments was county police Chief Tim Altomare. Chief Altomare has worked hard to restore the public trust damaged by a previous administration.

Police aren't being used for political purposes and the county executive hasn't used the police inappropriately — in fact, he has done just the opposite. Chief Altomare has made a genuine effort to build bridges and not walls.

Today, among other issues we will take up, we will request that the documentary "Walking Black" be shown to members of the chief's command staff.

"Walking Black" is a thought-provoking documentary on how to improve police and community relations. It was recently shown in Baltimore at the request of the mayor and led to broader discussions in the larger community.

Trust and accountability go hand in hand. Too often, politicians and bureaucrats forget that they are public servants. Their salaries, offices, cars and equipment are all paid for by taxpayers.

If you, just as I did, received your property tax bill, you know that the cost of government is ever-increasing. Therefore, it is imperative that citizens be kept informed on how their tax dollars are being prudently spent.

In a democracy, every four years voters have an opportunity to hire, rehire or fire their elected representatives. When transparency is the hallmark of an administration, the decision is easy.

Carl Snowden: Governor Hogan can end Anne Arundel court's shameful history

August 08, 2017

President Ronald Reagan appointed the first woman to the U.S. Supreme Court in 1981. His historic appointment of Associate Justice Sandra Day O'Connor paved the pathway for other women on the nation's highest court.

Today, there are three women serving on this nine-member body. Even the most sexist and bigoted critic would not claim that President Reagan was an extreme feminist.

Most reasonable people believe that the courts like the government should reflect the people that it serves and the taxpayers who subsidizes it.

There have been numerous demonstrations since January in front of the courthouse on Church Circle and at the Civil Rights Foot Soldiers Memorial across from the Arundel Center in Annapolis, protesting the execrable fact that the all-white Anne Arundel County Circuit Court must be changed to reflect the people that it serves. The protesters have been white, Asian, Latino, African-American and taxpayers.

In its over 366-years of existence, no Latino, Asian or African-American woman has ever served on the Anne Arundel County Circuit Court. In the State of Maryland, governors appoint people to serve on the circuit court.

Yet, regardless of the party of the governor, Democrat or Republican, no governor has ever appointed a black woman, Latino or Asian to serve. It did not make a difference, if the governor was a conservative or a liberal.

Only two African-American men have ever served on this court. One of them, Judge Clayton Greene, Jr., now serves on the Court of Appeals, Maryland's highest court.

The old stale argument that there are no "qualified" applicants is poppycock. A record number of applicants of color have applied.

Anne Arundel County is a diverse county and its diversity is growing every day. Taxpayers have a right to expect that their judiciary and their government reflect the people that it serves.

This evening, retired U.S. District Court Judge Alexander Williams, Jr. will be addressing the members of the Caucus of African American Leaders at 6 p.m. at the Wiley H. Bates Legacy Center, 1101 Smithville St. in Annapolis. The event is open to the public and free parking is in the rear of the building.

We invited the community to ask questions and learn how they can assist in ensuring that the courts reflect the people it serves.

Judge Williams is a highly respected jurist. A former Prince George County state's attorney and Howard University Law professor, Judge Williams will share his views on why it is important to have a diverse judiciary.

Gov. Larry Hogan like President Reagan with the stroke of a pen can bring to an end a shameful chapter in our county's history. There is simply no reason that people of color should not be serving on the County's circuit court.

Until, the courts and the government reflects the people that it serves, you can rest assured that we will continue to shout, *A Luta Continua*, which means in Portuguese the struggle continues for racial equality, justice and peace.

Carl Snowden: 2017 was the year local activism reignited

December 12, 2017

As we approach the end of the year, I am amazed at just how much has happened in 2017. Besides the obvious change — Annapolis' election of Mayor Gavin Buckley, which means a new first lady, Julie Williams Buckley — something else is happening: Activism is more intense than ever before.

After President Donald Trump was elected last year, activism reignited, and has become more focused than ever before.

Locally, new groups that have emerged include Action Annapolis, WISE, Showing Up for Racial Justice, Connecting the Dots, Coming to the Table, March on Maryland, the African Diaspora Identity Group and Anne Arundel Indivisible. These organizations — joined by the American Civil Liberties Union, the Caucus of African-American Leaders and the venerable NAACP — are energizing voters and citizens alike.

Some have appeared at meetings of the Anne Arundel County Council to protest new Chairman Michael Peroutka's association with alleged white supremacists and his support of the controversial Alabama U.S. Senate candidate Roy Moore.

They have shown up at the Anne Arundel County Circuit Court to protest an all-white judiciary and to call attention to hate crimes in the county. They have filed complaints with the Maryland Commission on Judicial Disabilities.

Several have appeared before the Annapolis City Council to complain about the disparate treatment of poor citizens.

Recently, the Caucus of African-American Leaders requested that U.S. Rep. John Sarbanes, D-Baltimore County, who represents Annapolis, have both the U.S. Departments of Justice and or Housing and Urban Development investigate policies by the Housing Authority of the City of Annapolis that permitted thousands of citizens' names and addresses to be given to the Annapolis Police Department in an effort to combat crime. This outrageous abuse of privacy demands answers.

The new activism can be felt at the polls. Many of these groups supported the successful candidacy of Mayor Gavin Buckley, who won by a landslide. The Caucus of African-American Leaders endorsed Mayor Buckley and seven of the eight victorious City Council candidates.

The caucus also received a commitment from these candidates to support their agenda, which is to preserve public housing for those who need it, create a civilian review board and ensure that the new administration reflects the community it serves.

This evening, Mayor Buckley and members of the City Council are expected to stop by at the monthly meeting of the Caucus of African-American Leaders to thank them for their support. The Caucus of African-American Leaders meets on the second Tuesday of each month at the Wiley H. Bates Legacy Center, 1101 Smithville St. in Annapolis. This meeting is open to the public as we continue to keep Dr. King's legacy alive. Review this!

The great abolitionist Frederick Douglass once said there where there is struggle, there is progress. If there's no struggle, there's no progress.

A Luta Continua, which in Portuguese means that the struggle for justice, freedom and peace continues!

Carl Snowden: Black history can be found on many street signs

February 13, 2018

Black history is an integral part of American history. Yet how many are truly aware of the contributions African-Americans have made to our city and society?

There are streets, roads, boulevards and highways named after famous African-Americans. Did you know that the state of Maryland and the city of Annapolis have numerous streets honoring African-Americans?

Many Americans are unaware that when President Donald Trump visits Bolling Air Force Base in Washington, D.C., he will be traveling on Malcolm X Avenue.

In Annapolis, thousands of motorists every day drive on Route 665, Aris T. Allen Boulevard. Many newcomers to this city and county are unaware that this boulevard is named after the only African-American to ever represent Anne Arundel County in the General Assembly, the late state Senator Aris T. Allen Sr., a prominent physician and politician. Sen. Allen was appointed to the state Senate, but had earlier been elected to the House of Delegates.

In the Eastport Terrace community, there are streets named after Frederick Douglass and Medgar Evers, respectively a great abolitionist and a civil rights icon. Before these streets were named, the mailing addresses for Eastport Terrace residents included only the name of the community. Almost 40 years ago, African-American activists were able to convince the city to name the streets in honor of these men.

In the Obery Court community, there is a street named after the late community activist Bertina Nick and the Abney family. Former Alderwoman Cynthia Abney Carter's family was one of the first families to move into the community, then called College Creek Terrace. Mrs. Carter was the first African-American woman elected to the Annapolis City Council. Her family was honored with a street named after them after College Creek Terrace and Obery Court were redeveloped.

In addition, Annapolis has a street named after Marion and George Phelps Jr., who were instrumental in shaping the civic affairs of our city.

Other streets named after African-Americans include Yevola S. Peters Way, Carroll Hynson Sr. Lane and, of course, Bates Street, named after the philanthropist and Alderman Wiley H. Bates. And there are other streets in the city named in honor of African-Americans.

It is important all our children know their history. The Anne Arundel County Public Schools should be teaching our children about Sarah Carter, the only African-American woman to ever serve on the Anne Arundel County Council.

Also, they should know who Walter Mills was and how he met Thurgood Marshall, who would later successfully sue the local school system on behalf of black teachers.

We will be celebrating black history and will be addressed by two candidates for governor: state Senator Richard Madaleno, and Baltimore County Executive Kevin B. Kamenetz. Please join us for an enlightening and informative meeting.

Carl Snowden: Historic injustice took 82 years to remedy

February 26, 2018

On Feb. 28, 1919, a 29-year-old man named John Snowden (no relation to me) was executed at Annapolis' old jail, which was on the site of today's Arundel Center. He was a black man who had been accused of raping and murdering a white woman in Annapolis.

John Snowden always maintained his innocence. An all-white jury deliberated for 20 minutes before convicting him and a judge sentenced him to hang.

Racial tensions in the city were heightened by the fact that just 13 years earlier a black man — Henry Davis, accused of assaulting a white woman — had been taken from that same jail by a mob and shot more than 100 times before being lynched. Gruesome photos of his mutilated body were sold as souvenirs.

In 1919, the overwhelming majority of African-Americans believed John Snowden was innocent. The Baltimore Sun reported that "as the execution date neared, Gov. Emerson Harrington rejected appeals for mercy … Annapolis was tense. The state militia patrolled black areas of the city, the Baltimore Police Department sent reinforcements and a machine gun detachment set up arms near the execution site."

On the day of the execution, a group of black women, all wearing white, left Asbury United Methodist Church on West Street and marched to the jail. They sang and prayed as the militia and police looked on.

Snowden's last statement was: "I have been imprisoned one year and six months and now I am about to shake hands with time and welcome eternity, for in a few hours from now I shall step out of time into eternity to pay the penalty of a crime I am not guilty of."

Hours after making that statement, he stood on the trap door. Before the executioner put the hood over his head and the noose around his neck, he joined the black women in singing "A Child of the King." After the executioner released the trap door, Snowden dangled from the noose for three agonizing minutes before being pronounced dead.

That evening, The Evening Capital received an anonymous letter from someone claiming the wrong man had been executed.

More than eight decades later, a group of concerned citizens organized a committee to look into the case. Those on that committee included Snowden's niece Hazel Snowden, Bishop Felton Edwin May, the Revs. Mamie A. Williams and Victor O. Johnson, George Phelps Jr., Janice Hayes-Williams, Jeffrey C. Henderson, Frederick C. Howard, Roger L. Murray Sr., Joy Bramble and me.

After letters were sent to then-Gov. Parris N. Glendening, he ordered an investigation by the Maryland Parole Commission, which did an exhaustive review of the documents, including court transcripts, government records and newspaper articles from the era. The commission recommended that the governor give a posthumous pardon to Snowden — something rarely done.

The governor signed that pardon on May 31, 2001. With the stroke of a pen, a historic injustice was righted.

Today, at the Brewer Hill Cemetery on West Street, there is a memorial plaque in memory of John Snowden, the last man executed in Annapolis. It's next to the memorial for Henry Davis. Both memorials are a reminder that an injustice need not be forever and that, in words with which the Rev. Martin Luther King Jr. often ended his speeches, "Truth crushed to the earth will rise again... and no lie can live forever."

We are eternally indebted to Gov. Glendening, who saw an injustice and acted. He knew, as we know, that you cannot change the past but you can learn from it.

John Snowden can now rest in peace because of Gov. Glendening. And somewhere in the heavens, Martin Luther King Jr. is looking down and saying, "Free at last, free at last, thank God almighty, he is free at last."

A Luta Continua, which in Portuguese means that the struggle for justice, freedom and peace continues!

Carl Snowden: Malcolm X has many lessons to teach us

May 21, 2018

May 19 would have been the 93rd birthday of someone who had an amazing impact on the world: Malcolm X.

Streets all over the world, including one leading to Andrews Air Force Base, are named for him. The same is true of schools. He's on postage stamps in the United States and other nations. A plaque in Annapolis honors him. Tre Williams, a student at Anne Arundel Community College, recently received the first Malcolm X Hero Award for saving the life of a Glen Burnie woman.

When I was a teenager attending Annapolis High School, I was required to read "The Autobiography of Malcolm X." That book changed my life forever. It was the first I read from cover to cover in one sitting. Malcolm's life story was phenomenal.

Here was a black boy, born May 19, 1925, who would become a world icon — one of the most respected human beings to ever occupy a leadership role in America — by the time he was assassinated on Feb. 21, 1965.

His searing analysis of the issue of racism was second to none. He openly talked about the mistakes he made and the lessons he learned.

Malcolm dropped out of the eighth grade after receiving a racial slur from a teacher. After dropping out of school, Malcom was later incarcerated. While in prison, he discovered books and the power of knowledge. He once said that information is the most lethal weapon a human being can have. He knew his history and, more importantly, how to apply it. It was Malcolm X who taught me that Nat Turner was not insane but a patriot who, like Patrick Henry, wanted freedom.

One of the most important lessons Malcolm X taught me was the value of time. Those who attend the Caucus of African-American Leaders' monthly meetings know I believe in beginning and ending meetings on time. Time is a precious commodity. Once used, it can never be retrieved. Like youth, it is finite. One day you will look back on your life and discover that you have used it either wisely or foolishly.

The other great lesson Malcolm taught me was to think for myself and not allow others to define me. When I am criticized, I remember that Malcolm X said, "If those in the power structure are patting you on the back, you must be doing something wrong".

I do not need other people's validation. I am quite comfortable with who I am and what I believe.

I have had the great joy of being able to travel the world and to meet many people from different cultures and backgrounds. I appreciate how much human beings have in common. Regardless of their religion, nationality, gender, sexual orientation or ideology, their common denominator is that thing we call death. No one is here forever; everyone is allotted a certain amount of time. Malcolm understood that. What you choose to do with the allotted time is up to you.

Malcolm X once said, "A person who does not know their history is like a tree without roots; they are bound to perish." On May 28 I will be doing a free walking tour, open to anyone who wants to attend, of African-American historic sites in Annapolis. It will begin at 10 a.m. at the Civil Rights Foot Soldiers Memorial, across from the Arundel Center, 44 Calvert St. Please wear casual clothing and comfortable shoes.

Malcolm X also once said, "Do you know why the sun rises in the east and sets in the west? ... Pick up a book and you will learn." I picked up the "Autobiography of Malcolm X" and now I know. You will, too, if you take this tour on May 28.

A Luta Continua, which means that the struggle continues.

Carl Snowden: City Council deserves credit for acknowledging a painful, long-ignored truth

June 25, 2018

The Annapolis City Council last week passed a historic resolution that recognized the truth Malcolm X and Martin Luther King Jr. spoke of: No lie can live forever.

This was the first in a series of steps the city needs to take to recognize that citizens and visitors alike are better served when we recognize historic wrongs by creating a contemporaneous plan that restores justice.

The resolution, "Recognizing and Remembering Racial Injustice — An Apology," was sponsored by Alderwomen Elly Tierney and Rhonda Pindell Charles and co-sponsored by all seven of their colleagues, including Mayor Gavin Buckley.

It came 120 years after a white mob broke into the County Jail on Calvert Street — now the site of the Arundel Center — and lynched Wright Smith, a black man accused but never tried on charges of assaulting two white women.

This was no one-time event. In 1906, Henry Davis, another black man accused of assaulting a white woman, was also lynched by a mob. The Evening Capital referred to Davis as a "Negro brute" but also condemned the lynching, saying it had given Anne Arundel County "a black eye."

An unsympathetic New York Times editorial said, "What the lynchers killed was merely a Negro, who seems thoroughly to have deserved the killing." Such were the attitudes of that era. Altogether, there were over 4,700 documented lynchings in the United States.

The Henry Davis Memorial in West Street's Brewer Hill Cemetery is the only memorial to the victims of lynchings in our county. Those who spearheaded the effort that led to that memorial, dedicated in 2001 by then-Mayor Ellen O. Moyer, hoped it would help educate future generations.

Sadly, this hasn't happened. Anne Arundel County Public Schools doesn't have field trips to the Davis memorial. Students graduating from our local public schools and colleges have no idea these horrific lynchings occurred in this city.

Don't believe me? Ask recent graduates of our high schools, Anne Arundel Community College, St. John's College or the Naval Academy. Their ignorance on this subject is exceeded only by their general lack of knowledge of American history.

Annapolis prides itself on history and tourism, but this isn't the history visitors are told or students are taught.

On Memorial Day, I gave a tour on the history of black Annapolis. We chose Memorial Day because it's the holiday on which we pause to honor those who have died in war. And our continuing fight against racism is one of our great wars.

When the tour visited the Davis memorial, those taking part — black, white and Latino — were mesmerized to hear how Davis had been shot over 100 times by a mob near St. John's College, and how an enterprising white man took photos of the mutilated body and sold postcards as souvenirs.

It is difficult to accept that your ancestors may have been involved in barbaric acts. Yet these lynchings were done in public. No one was ever arrested, prosecuted or convicted for these crimes. When they occurred, city officials refused to condemn them. And Annapolitans, for the most part, remained silent.

Some believe no good can be gained by bringing up Annapolis' dark past. I disagree. I commend the City Council for passing this resolution.

On many of the tombstones in cemeteries like Brewer Hill you see the words "rest in peace." But there can be no peace until there is justice. And justice and peace begin the day we recognize that, as the author and novelist James Baldwin once wrote, "Not everything that is faced can be changed, but nothing can be changed until it is faced."

Carl Snowden: Remember ancestors at local memorial

July 23, 2018

If you visit the Civil Rights Foot Soldiers Memorial just before sunrise or sunset, or if you go at a time when there is less traffic, and you take a moment to meditate or pray, you may hear the voices of our ancestors.

I am aware there are people who do not believe God exists, but my experience is that God does exist and he allows our ancestors to speak to us.

As I looked at the names on the memorial of the many people who affected our community both locally and nationally, I marveled over the fact that most were just ordinary men and women whose contributions, in part, were doing their share.

Some walked, some marched, some ran, some talked, some sang, some led, some gave money, some died, but all contributed something. This memorial should serve as a reminder that we all have a responsibility to do our "something."

There are five things I recommend we all do.

One, vote. Perhaps, of all of the hard-gained victories, this is the most important.

We have a primary in the city of Annapolis on Tuesday. Please vote and remember why there are those who want to suppress your vote. Your vote is why President Barack Obama was in the White House and three African-Americans are on the City Council.

Second, join the NAACP. Started more than a century ago, it is the oldest civil rights organization in America. There is strength in numbers. The NAACP remains the oldest and largest civil rights organization in our community and we must support it with our membership.

Third, emphasize to our children the importance of education. In the years to come, education will be the key to their progress. Make no mistake about it. The late Whitney Young of the National Urban League once observed, "It is better to be prepared and not have an opportunity, than to have an opportunity and not be prepared."

When I was growing up my elders told me the following, "Boy, get a good education, it is the one thing that they cannot take from you." That was quickly followed by this sage advice, "You have to be twice as smart to get half as far..." Believe me, I know what they meant.

Fourth, it is not the responsibility of the government or of white folks to raise our children. This is our responsibility. When I see our children and grandchildren going astray, I blame the elders.

Far too many of us are not willing to take on this responsibility, and neither space nor time allows me to expound more on this subject, but I believe the Rev. Jesse Jackson got it right when he said, "Nobody will save us, from us, for us, but us."

Fifth, at many of our community rallies you will notice I often asked people to join hands and then turn to one another and simply say, "I love you." The purpose of this exercise is to remind each of us that despite our differences on issues and petty disputes, in the final analysis, we must demonstrate a love for each other that will transcend the moment.

On the Civil Rights Foot Soldiers Memorial you will find inscribed the names of the late Rev. Ralph David Abernathy, Malcolm X, Dr. Dorothy Irene Height, Rosa Parks, Coretta Scott King, James Baldwin, Congressman Adam Clayton Powell Jr. and many other famous national personalities.

The one thing they have in common with the local leaders such as the Rev. Leroy Bowman, Judge Mary Sellman Jackson, Lulu P. Hardesty, Walter Blasingame, Father David H. Croll, Alderman Samuel Gilmer, the Rev. Mildred Holliday and others, is that if you take the time to look up their history, they all did their "something." They all became history makers because they were not excuse makers.

Every man and woman on the Civil Rights Foot Soldiers Memorial did something to improve the plight of their community.

The future of the next generation is dependent upon us doing our "something." If the five recommendations I have made are not enough, please suggest and then do the sixth or seventh. And then your ancestors, either early in the morning or late at night, will whisper "thank you" to you.

Carl Snowden: Local or national, sex scandals are nothing new

November 28, 2018

Sex scandals, sexual harassment and sexual assaults have dominated the headlines recently. This sell newspapers and guarantees more television viewers. The more sensational the scandal, the better.

Hardly a day goes by without a new sex scandal. And every time, it serves to renew the demand for more action on the part of our elected officials.

The philosopher George Santayana said, "Those who cannot remember the past are condemned to repeat it." He was right! Reading today's headlines regarding sex scandals, younger readers may have concluded this is a new phenomenon. It is not.

This is from an article in The Baltimore Sun on Dec. 10, 1991, regarding a sex scandal involving the Annapolis Fire Department: "An Annapolis firefighter fired after being accused of having sex on duty was reinstated yesterday after the city attorney learned that a fire department investigator on the case once had sex with the woman described as 'central to the allegations.'"

You read that correctly. The investigator had sex with the person that he was investigating. You cannot make this stuff up.

This was a huge scandal at the time; I was a member of the Annapolis City Council when the story broke. Firefighters were disciplined and elected officials said steps were being taken to make sure it would never happen again.

Of course, no matter how often elected officials say that, sex scandals never end.

This county had an infamous one involving then-County Executive John Leopold. The Washington Post wrote on Feb. 19, 2009: "The Anne Arundel County Council is summoning Police Chief James Teare Sr. to answer questions about how officers handled a report about alleged sexual behavior in the county executive's official car at an Annapolis parking lot."

Mr. Leopold, who was convicted of misconduct, resigned in 2013. While he was not convicted of having sex on the job, his alleged conduct did lead to his resignation. A Capital story earlier this month indicated that Mr. Leopold may be planning to run for public office once again.

Sex scandals — whether the one involving then-President Bill Clinton, a Democrat, or then-Alabama Gov. Robert Bentley, a Republican — have tainted public officials of both parties and their legacies.

Maryland is no exception; there have been sex scandals involving both political parties in our state as well. Governors, members of Congress and local elected officials have not been immune.

Now, as a result of new controversies involving Alabama U.S. Senate candidate Roy Moore and Minnesota's Democratic U.S. Sen. Al Franken, voters will once again be faced with choices about who they want to represent them.

Last year, the electorate voted for President Donald Trump despite a videotape of him boasting that he could get away with sexual misbehavior. The voters also elected and re-elected Bill Clinton, before the Monica Lewinsky scandal led to his impeachment, but after such questions had already been raised about his conduct.

In a few weeks, we will know whether voters in Alabama will be as forgiving. Also, we will know whether Santayana was correct that those who don't remember the past are doomed to repeat it.

What do you think? Will voters, male and female, forgive a candidate who has groped individuals? How about one accused by multiple women of having solicited minors for sex? And what, if anything, will other elected officials on the national, state and local levels do about this tawdry behavior?

A Luta Continua, which in Portuguese means that the struggle for justice, freedom and peace continues!

Carl Snowden: Malcolm X remains an inspiration

February 09, 2019

The 1960s were probably the most significant decade in American history. Arguably, it had the most impact on the civil rights movement. It was a tumultuous time. In that decade we saw the assassinations of Mississippi NAACP leader Medgar Evers, President John F. Kennedy, Malcolm X, Martin Luther King Jr. and Sen. Robert F. Kennedy; all within five years. Each of those assassinations changed the course of history.

Malcolm X became an iconic figure. Like Dr. King, he holds a unique position in American history. This Feb. 21 marks the 50th anniversary of his assassination.

It is an assassination that remains controversial. While there is no debate that members of the Nation of Islam murdered Malcolm, there remain many unanswered questions surrounding who ordered his death. More than one attempt was made on his life. Malcolm, like Dr. King, was under surveillance by the CIA, the FBI and the State Department. They both were targets of the FBI's COINTELPRO, the government's counterintelligence program.

On Feb. 21 there will be a forum at the Wiley H. Bates Legacy Center in Annapolis looking at Malcolm X's life and legacy. Time magazine called "The Autobiography of Malcolm X" one of the most important books published in the 20th century. President Obama indicated that this book had a profound impact on him. It changed my life.

Few individuals have had the impact on our society, as did Malcolm X. The late Alex Haley, who co-wrote Malcolm's autobiography, told me it was Malcolm X who influenced him to write his bestseller "Roots." Malcolm's influence can be seen in movies and pop culture, and his image is known all over the world. Long before the United States decided to create a postage stamp in his honor, nations in Africa and the Middle East had already done so.

Anne Arundel County has a special connection to the legacy of Malcolm X. Two of his six daughters and a grandson have spoken here in the county. Ilyasah Shabazz keynoted a Dr. Martin Luther King, Jr. Awards Dinner and Attallah Shabazz, his oldest daughter, addressed Anne Arundel County Public School students on a visit here. Malcolm Shabazz, his grandson, addressed an audience at the Wiley H. Bates Legacy Center on the occasion of Malcolm X's birthday. Ironically and sadly, Malcolm's grandson was murdered in Mexico not long after his appearance in the county.

Malcolm X has meant many things to many people. The late New York Times writer M.S. Handler wrote, "No man in our time aroused fear and hatred in the white man as did Malcolm, because in him the white man sensed an implacable foe who could not be had for any price — a man unreservedly committed to the cause of liberating the black man in American society rather than integrating the black man into that society."

The great actor Ossie Davis, in Malcolm's eulogy said, "Here at this final hour, in this quiet place, Harlem has come to bid farewell to one of its brightest hopes — extinguished now, and gone forever".

One would assume that a half-century later, this man, who never held public office nor met with a U.S. president might have been forgotten. Yet, it is these words that were spoken by Ossie Davis at Malcolm's funeral that will ensure his place in history. Mr. Davis said, "For if you did you would know him. And if you knew him you know why we must honor him: Malcolm was our manhood, our living, black manhood! This was his meaning to his people, and in honoring him, we honor the best in ourselves." He further stated "and we will know him then for what he was and is — a prince — our own black shining prince, who didn't hesitate to die, because he loved us so."

During Black History Month, President Obama and Gov. Larry Hogan have issued proclamations urging citizens to celebrate the contributions of African-Americans, I would recommend that readers read "The Autobiography of Malcolm X" so you too may understand why Malcolm continues to inspire people around the world.

Carl Snowden: We are all 'involved in mankind'

November 24, 2015

In two days, we will be celebrating the Thanksgiving holiday. This celebration comes on the heels of a bombing in Paris and the recent announcement that Baltimore's homicide rate for this year has reached more than 300 people.

The great cities of Paris and Baltimore both have suffered death and destruction. Thousands of miles apart, they are both part of the human family.

English poet John Donne, put it this way: "No man is an island, entire of itself; every man is a piece of the continent, a part of the main." He further wrote, "Any man's death diminishes me, because I am involved in mankind; and therefore never send to know for whom the bell tolls; it tolls for thee."

People dying on the streets of France and America — "senseless" is the word most often use to describe the carnage. Mothers burying their children. Fathers experiencing pain and grief.

I have had an opportunity to see a lot of the world that we live in. I have traveled to Africa, Europe, Central America and the Middle East.

I have seen firsthand this magnificent world with all its splendor. I have seen peace and I have seen war. I have seen the dichotomy and pell-mell of life.

My mother, who next year will turn 100 years old, has seen less of the world than I, but the wisdom that she has acquired has help me to better understand the human experience.

As I get older, it seems that the elderly are required to leave their wisdom for the generations that will follow, a wisdom that seeks the greater good.

As families gather around their dining tables on Thanksgiving Day, giving thanks for the blessings that they have received, here is a thought I would like for them to consider.

Water is essential in life; without it, there is no life. It is interesting that while there are different bodies of water — e.g., oceans, lakes, streams, ponds — they all flow together. They serve humankind and nature.

As we see religious and political strife throughout the world, it would be so wonderful if people could be like the bodies of water — not in conflict, but existing to serve humankind.

History is replete with religious wars. It is my hope that one day humankind will learn to be one with nature and, like water, find that God has a place for everyone.

It is my prayer that although there remain wars, poverty, and racism, your Thanksgiving holiday will allow you to take just a moment to remember the words of John Donne: "Any man's death diminishes me, because I am involved in mankind."

This Thanksgiving the people of Paris and Baltimore need both our prayers and our commitment to make the world a better place.

A Luta Continua, which in Portuguese means that the struggle continues!

Carl Snowden: My mother has seen the dream get nearer

The late Ora Snowden, the mother of the author.

Jan 12, 2016

On a Wednesday in 1916, as recorded by the certificate issued by Maryland's Division of Vital Records, a "Negro" was born. The baby girl's father and mother were classified in the same way, and this would be a determining factor in the life of this child.

Today, we are celebrating our mother, Ora Brown Snowden's 100th birthday. We as a family are blessed to have a matriarch who has lived long enough to see a century of change.

Our mother was born in the presidency of Woodrow Wilson, 13 years before Martin Luther King Jr. She was born before women had the right to vote, went through the Great Depression and innumerable wars, and seen President Barack Obama, an African-American, elected president. She has seen gay marriage, consumer rights and an environmental justice and a civil rights movement that changed America forever.

This Friday, at the 28th Annual Dr. Martin Luther King, Jr. Awards Dinner at the La Fontaine Bleue in Glen Burnie, I plan to pay a special tribute to her.

In many ways, my mom's life has reflected what Dr. King gave his life for. She was part of a generation that at birth was being denied basic civil rights. There were restrictions on where she could live, who she could marry, where her children could attend school and where she could eat — all based on her color.

Our mother is old enough to remember the segregated movie theaters in Annapolis. She remembers restaurants that wouldn't serve African-Americans. Revisionists would have you believe that before the 1964 Civil Rights Act became law of the land, blacks in Annapolis were dining in white restaurants. Not true!

She remembers when African-Americans were not allowed to have babies at the old Anne Arundel General Hospital on South Street.

Our mother saw an apartheid system collapse under marching feet and praying hands. She saw millions of disenfranchised Americans win the right to vote. In the words of the Rev. Jesse Jackson, "hands that once picked cotton, now pick presidents."

Ora Snowden has seen many demonstrations, including Ku Klux Klan demonstrations, in our capital city. She has seen the greatness of America, and seen America at its lowest points. She lived through the bombing of the Baptist Church in Birmingham, Alabama, that took the life of four innocent little girls. She experienced the horrific assassinations of NAACP leader Medgar Evers, President John F. Kennedy, Malcolm X, Martin Luther King Jr. and Sen. Robert F. Kennedy. She saw Nelson Mandela walk out of a prison cell in South Africa, then become the president of the Republic of South Africa.

Ora's children are all now adults; she has lived long enough to see her grandchildren, great-grandchildren and great-great-grandchildren come into a world changed by Dr. King and the civil rights movement.

Not many are blessed to become a centenarian. Our mom is one of them. She is in reasonably good health. Her memory is excellent.

On her birthday, I wanted to make sure that, unlike the day she was born, we would take notice not of a "Negro" but of a human being whose life has inspired many. Her family and friends have found in this woman an example of not just longevity, but what it means to survive against the odds. Maya Angelou would refer to her and other women like her as "phenomenal" and remind the world, that "still we rise."

Our mother is a strong woman of faith. Like Dr. King, she, too, saw a better America on the horizon and, like Dr. King, she never lost faith in her people or her nation.

On Friday, when we celebrate the birthday of Dr. King, we will have with us a living example of how his life made a difference. When you hear my mother say, *A Luta Continua*, which in Portuguese means "the struggle continues," it will not be a motto, but a reminder that we are closer to Dr. King's dream than ever before.

Carl Snowden: County executives leave legacies

June 14, 2016

Muhammad Ali was undoubtedly one of the most colorful and important figures of the 20th century. He won his first heavyweight championship in the same year charter government came to Anne Arundel County. Like Ali, the early county executives didn't realize the extent of the legacy they would leave.

Several weeks ago, I ran into Robert A. Pascal, the second county executive and thought about his legacy and those of the other county executives. I have worked with every one of them since charter government — some very good, some very bad.

The first, Joseph W. Alton Jr., was popular, but threatened to demolish the old Mount Moriah African Methodist Episcopal Church on Franklin Street in Annapolis. I remember, as a teenager, demonstrating in front of the Arundel Center with Walter Blasingame and others from the NAACP to preserve the church — even as Mr. Alton said he would personally bulldoze it and was willing to go to jail if that's what it took to demolish the building.

As fate would have it, eventually, Alton went to jail for trying to get kickbacks, and not for demolishing the church — now the site of the Banneker-Douglass Museum.

Several buildings in the county have Pascal's name on them. He, too, was popular, particularly with senior citizens, and served two successful terms. He was followed by O. James Lighthizer, the first Democrat in the post, whose most foremost legacy, in my opinion, is Quiet Waters Park.

I was on the Annapolis City Council when Mayor Dennis M. Callahan wanted to annex the property for a housing development, expanding the tax base. I remember the controversy well. Every time I visit Quiet Waters Park, with my granddaughter and her pet dog, Precious, I'm impressed anew by the gift Lighthizer left for future generations.

Lighthizer was followed for one term by Robert Neall, a well-known fiscal conservative who was a Republican at the time but later became a Democrat. We got along fine. Next was Republican John Gary, another one-term executive. In 1994, he joined me, U.S. Sen. Barbara Mikulski, Gov. Parris Glendening and over 1,000 citizens in a march to protest the Ku Klux Klan – a sight to behold.

Next was Democrat Janet S. Owens, the first woman county executive, whose accomplishments I saw firsthand, as I served in her Cabinet. I remember when Mrs. Owens abolished the adopt-a-road program rather than allow the Ku Klux Klan to join it. The African-American community will always remember that it was under Owens that the Kunta Kinte-Alex Haley Memorial on the City Dock was created, the old Wiley H. Bates High School was preserved and the Dr. Martin Luther King, Jr. Memorial was created at Anne Arundel Community College.

Next was Republican John R. Leopold, who became the first county executive to resign in disgrace. Leopold compiled dossiers on political opponents, including me. With the assistance of the American Civil Liberties Union, I sued Mr. Leopold and he became the only county executive held personally liable in a civil suit for his misdeeds.

Next was Laura Neuman, who completed Mr. Leopold's unfinished second term and helped establish the Civil Rights Foot Soldiers Memorial directly across from the Arundel Center in Whitmore Park.

The Caucus of African-American Leaders meets on the second Tuesday of each month at the Wiley H. Bates Legacy Center, 1101 Smithville St. in Annapolis. This meeting is open to the public as we continue to keep Dr. King's legacy alive.

What will Mr. Schuh's legacy be? Affordable housing? Better schools? Addressing systemic racism in county government? A countywide mass transit system? Getting local government to reflect the citizens it serves?

Tonight, citizens will have an opportunity to ask the county executive anything they like. Mr. Schuh's legacy is a work in progress, and tonight, by questioning him, we will have an opportunity to help shape it.

Carl Snowden: Remembering my friend Alan Legum

Aug 23, 2016

Tick, tock, tick, tock. Sometimes the clock of life stops ticking. Sue Mann, a friend and a legal secretary called me to share the sad news that our friend Alan H. Legum, a prominent Annapolis civil rights lawyer, had died. At that moment, my world came to a standstill.

Alan was my friend, my lawyer and one of my most trusted confidants. He was an integral part of my life. We shared a bond born out of struggle, a friendship that was never breached.

I immediately thought about the last of our many lunches together. He shared with me that he was going to have an operation and talked about the success rate of such procedures. He told me very calmly and deliberately, that he hoped it would go well.

Then he talked about how, over the years, we had worked on numerous civil rights cases. He talked about our first successful case against the FBI, which had illegally created a dossier on me because of my political views. Alan had not been practicing long then. I was one of his first clients and this was his first case in U.S. District Court. He took on the U.S. Department of Justice and its vast army of lawyers and won — a small Annapolis law firm beating the federal government.

Alan eloquently reminded the court that in America the First Amendment protected free speech and was the cornerstone of our democracy. The judge ordered the FBI to expunge my file, and pay me a monetary settlement and attorney fees.

Alan never once boasted about this victory. He just said we had a good case. This became the catalyst for a friendship that would last more than 40 years.

At that last lunch, he also talked about his family. He told me how much he loved his wife Emily. He told me how fortunate we both were to be grandfathers. He shared his admiration for his sons Judd and Adam. Frequently, when Judd would appear on television or write a commentary, Alan would proudly send me the information.

When the lunch ended, he stood up, shook my hand and said, "I will always treasure our friendship." I had no idea how important those words would be to me.

Last weekend, on a sweltering summer Sunday, hundreds, including many dignitaries, gathered at Overlook Park to say goodbye. Invited to speak by Judd Legum, I had spent a lot of time putting together my remarks. I wanted to share with them the Alan Legum that I knew:

The man who was the epitome of integrity, effectively representing people living in dystopian subsidized housing who had been on a rent strike for more than 18 months. The man who won two class action employment racial discrimination cases against the City of Annapolis, giving people of color the opportunity to be promoted in the police and fire departments. The man who was successful in getting the first African-American deputy fire chief, Gregory Lawrence, reinstated at the BWI Thurgood Marshall Airport Fire Department.

Because of Alan's support and efforts that we have a Dr. Martin Luther King, Jr. Memorial at Anne Arundel Community College, a Coretta Scott King Memorial Garden in Edgewater and the Civil Rights Foot Soldiers Memorial in Annapolis. For all three, provided legal services and financial support.

And through my own trials and tribulations, he stood with me. I wanted that audience to know that he was the kind of person they would be happy to call friend.

Alan and I never talked about what would happen if either of us passed before the other. I shared with the audience that during the annual Dr. Martin Luther King, Jr. Awards Dinner, which Alan, always attended, we will be giving an annual Alan Hilliard Legum Humanitarian Award.

I will forever treasure this friendship and will spend the rest of my life, struggling to create a world where there are more people like Alan Legum — people who believe in justice for all and live their lives in such a manner. Tick, tock, tick, tock.

A Luta Continua, which in Portuguese means that the struggle continues.

Carl Snowden: Legalizations of 'vices' have a racial angle

September 13, 2016

History has a way of repeating itself. I have met some colorful characters in my life. One was the Little Willie Adams. I first met him in 1971; he was in the "numbers" business.

He was a prominent businessman with an interest in a number of local African-American businesses, including the old Carr's Beach. When he died at age 97, The Baltimore Sun called him a "venture capitalist."

When I was growing up in Annapolis, many of the number runners were African-American. Numbers was a cash cow, so widely played in the black community at the time that both preachers and politicians benefited from it. Many churches benefited from the generosity of the winners and politicians ranging from governors to local legislators gladly received donations from these sources.

Numbers was a major business, a racket, an illegal form of gambling. It was tax-free. It employed many people, generating dollars that were used to start many black businesses. Believe it or not, Annapolis had more African-American businesses in the 1960s, than it does today.

I remember that when I was a child people found out what the number for that day was by word of mouth. You did not look for the numbers on television or newspapers. Amazingly, in less than 24 hours an entire community was informed of the number for that day.

When the state decided to get in to the numbers business — i.e., the state's lottery — African-Americans were the real losers. Gone were the black "bankers," the number runners and, yes, the "investors." As the state took over this enterprise, the illicit capital that was used to underwrite some black businesses was lost — at a time when, because of redlining and other discriminatory practices, African-Americans did not have access to many of the banks.

The numbers business was replaced with the state's official gaming system, which had few blacks in significant positions. Black "bankers" were replaced by white "managers," and the political influence of those blacks waned as well.

Now, here is where history repeats itself. The Capital recently published the list of licenses for the new marijuana distributors and, yes, African-Americans are conspicuously absent.

Do you know how many black so-called drug dealers were sent to jail over the last three decades for what now will become a legitimate enterprise? Do you have any idea of the number of young black men's lives and families that were destroyed for allegedly selling and smoking weed?

During Mr. Adams' era, he understood power and racism. He knew the system was dominated by whites and knew full well the mythology of capitalism.

The late U.S. Rep. Parren J. Mitchell was fond of saying, if you don't understand racism, "you are either dumbfounded or founded dumb." Del. Kenneth L. Webster once said, "If your hair is knotty and your nose is snotty and you don't know, ask somebody."

Perhaps, now is the time to ask some questions. As the use of marijuana becomes a legal commodity, what will happen to all those people who were arrested and received criminal records? What will be done in the name of justice for these people?

Speaking of justice, I did note that one of the local investors whose group received a permit from the state was former Sheriff George F. Johnson, IV. Twenty years ago, he was arresting people who smoked marijuana. Now he and his fellow investors will be making a profit from the same enterprise that black people went to jail for.

I thank my elders for educating me so that I understood very well why a black man's enterprise of selling drugs became the target of a "war on drugs" and why a white man's enterprise of selling the same drugs is a "capitalist venture."

Carl Snowden: Looking back on 2016, a year of highs, lows

December 27, 2016

In just four days, we will be welcoming a new year, 2017. However, before we say goodbye to 2016, I just wanted to share some observations about the high and low points the year had for me.

One of my great joys this year was to be able to celebrate my mother's 100th birthday in January at the annual Dr. Martin Luther King Jr. Awards Dinner and Reception at the La Fontaine Bleue in Glen Burnie. Hundreds gathered to celebrate the birthdays of the Rev. King and my mom. What a joy to participate in this celebration. On Jan. 13 next month, we hope to once again celebrate both her and the Rev. King's birthdays.

One of my lowest points was the death of my friend Alan Legum. He was my confidant, lawyer and trusted ally. One of the things that I most enjoyed doing with Alan was reading books and then discussing them over a leisurely lunch.

We read the trilogy of Taylor Branch's books on Rev. King, Malcolm X and the civil rights movement. We would spend time reflecting on where the nation was headed. He would share with me his love for his family and his wife Emily. I would tell him about my sons and how they were progressing. We would talk about politics and current events.

When Alan died earlier this year, with the permission of his family, we created an award in his name that will be given at both the Dr. Martin Luther King Jr. Awards Dinner and the breakfast held at Anne Arundel Community College.

This was also the year that, as of this writing, 10 homicides occurred in Annapolis — a record, and something that every Annapolitan knows is unacceptable. Many of the victims were young people. Their families will always remember 2016 as the year they did not spend Christmas with their loved ones.

Politics, a staple in this town, was going full blast. The 2016 presidential election was filled with some of the most coarse and uncivil discourse that I had ever heard. Women were demeaned, Latinos were insulted, the disabled were made fun of and Donald J. Trump still won, despite all of this. Next month he will be inaugurated as the 45th president of the United States.

I suspect the great wall that he promised to build will go the way of "a chicken in every pot and a car in every garage" that Herbert Hoover promised when he won the presidency in 1928. We all know how that turned out.

Democrats won in Anne Arundel County by a slim margin, but by a huge one in Annapolis, where Hillary Clinton carried the city by 62 percent.

Now, Annapolis voters are preparing for municipal elections next year. As in the presidential election, this local election will have citizens engaged as never before. There is a lot at stake.

We also witnessed some progress this year. The Caucus of African-American Leaders, the NAACP and the American Civil Liberties Union were able to get the Annapolis Police Department to do a pilot body camera program. We saw area churches seeking to bring people together to improve race relations in the city and county.

Yes, 2016, has been a year of great joy and sadness. Yet, I have faith in the future.

I know that we as a nation will be faced with many challenges. I am well aware that these challenges will be both painful and powerful — painful because they will involve issues that we thought were long resolved, powerful because we will see in Annapolis a reawakening of activism.

To all who read this column: I wish you and your family a happy new year, filled with promise and hope — a new year that reminds us all that life is short, so you should enjoy every minute you can with a loved one.

Carl Snowden: Answer to uncertainty is prayer

January 24, 2017

At 12:01 p.m. on Jan. 20, the historic and meaningful Obama era came to an end. Years from now, Americans will look back at this era as one of the great milestones in their history.

President Barack Obama was given credit for averting a financial crisis when he came into office. He saved the auto industry and restored confidence in the economy. Gas prices went down.

Obama's election and re-election were among the great joys in my life. Former County Councilman Daryl Jones and I went to the White House and had an opportunity to see the Naval Academy football team lauded by President Obama. He was as warm and personable in person as he is on television. His smile is contagious.

I know that President Obama had both admirers and detractors. I remember reading Colbert I. King's column, headlined "A dangerous kind of hate," which appeared in The Washington Post in September 2009. King quoted the Rev. Steven I. Anderson of Faithful Word Baptist Church in Temple, Arizona, who preached a sermon titled, "Why I Hate Barack Obama."

"I'm not going to pray for his good," King quoted Anderson as saying. "I'm going to pray that he dies and goes to hell." He also reportedly said: "I'd like him to die of natural causes. I don't want him to be a martyr. We don't need another holiday. I'd like see him to die, like Ted Kennedy, of brain cancer."

The Rev. Anderson wanted Michelle Obama to become a widow like Jacqueline Kennedy. You might dismiss him as just another right-wing bigot, but he was not alone. According to that same column, the Rev. Wiley Drake of First Southern Baptist Church in Buena Park, California, was also praying for President Obama's early demise.

The hatred of some toward President Obama was exceeded only by their disrespect. How well I remember U.S. Rep. Joe Wilson, R-South Carolina, shouting "You lie" at the president during a State of the Union address. There were countless other examples of an ugliness that was disgraceful.

But those of us, who had seen bullets and not ballots change the course of history were praying also. Every night, we would pray to God that President Obama not suffer the same fate as President John F. Kennedy, Malcolm X, Martin Luther King Jr. or Sen. Robert F. Kennedy.

In our churches, temples, mosques and synagogues we prayed that the bigots who screamed "We want our country back" wouldn't succeed. I remember vividly when a group of ministers surrounded the president in 2012 and prayed for him.

I will never forget the eulogy President Obama gave in South Carolina after the murder of nine people at Emanuel African Methodist Episcopal Church in 2015. When he ended his remarks with the song "Amazing Grace," I felt a relief come over me that I am sure was shared by all those who were watching.

Now that the Obama presidency has ended and his beautiful daughters, wife and mother-in-law have left the White House, I will continue to pray for the new occupant of the White House. I will pray for President Donald Trump and his family and for our nation. We are about to enter an era that has already created anxiety and anguish.

There is great uncertainty in the air. Will there be a war? Will there be unrest? Where are we headed? These and many more questions are being asked. The answer to all of them is prayer.

I remember being told by the late Rev. Leroy Bowman of First Baptist Church in Annapolis that praying and crying are good for the soul: "Brother Carl, crying is God's way of letting us know that we are human. Praying is our way of letting God know that we know that he is in charge." Keep the faith. Keep hope alive.

That sage counsel allows me to end this column with *A Luta Continua*, which in Portuguese means "the struggle continues."

Carl Snowden: Play offers a view of what might have been

May 08, 2017

The Rev. Martin Luther King Jr. once said, "Tomorrow is today. We are confronted with the fierce urgency of now. In this unfolding conundrum of life and history, there is such a thing as being too late."

History is replete with examples of the ominous "too late" syndrome. Historians and others have often wondered what life might have been like if certain events had not intervened in our lives.

It was Malcolm X who reminded us that bullets, not ballots, have often changed the course of history. So many of us wonder what might have happen if President John F. Kennedy had not been assassinated in 1963.

What would have happened if the brother of President Kennedy, Sen. Robert F, Kennedy, had not have been slain in California in 1968, or if the Rev. King had not been killed that same year?

There is a famous photograph of the Rev. King and Malcolm X shaking hands and smiling. It was taken in Washington, D.C., where these two iconic figures accidentally met for the first time. Photographers and journalists captured this moment in history.

It is a special moment. It is a moment that has come to symbolize what might have been.

It is a unity without uniformity — Malcolm and Martin shaking hands. They are smiling. No one will ever know what was going through their minds on that fateful day.

Within four years of that meeting in Washington, D.C., both of them, at age 39, would become victims of assassins' bullets, Malcolm in Harlem in New York City, Martin in Memphis, Tennessee. These bullets decided the course of a nation.

What might have been? If these two had an opportunity to talk, what would they have said to each other? Would the Christian and the Muslim have shared religious views? Would these two activists have talked about strategy? Would these men talk about their families?

A play, "The Meeting," by Jeff Stetson, is a fictional account of what these two men might have talked about had they met prior to their assassinations. In the play, the meeting takes place in a hotel room in Harlem in 1965.

The play will be performed this evening at the Caucus of African-American Leaders' monthly meeting, beginning at 5 at the historic Wiley H. Bates Legacy Center, 1101 Smithville Street, Annapolis. There is no admission charge. The meeting is open to the public and complimentary food and beverages will be provided.

Carltaise Ransom will play Malcolm X, Curtis McNeil will play the Rev. King and George Oliver Buntin will play Rashad, Malcolm's trusted bodyguard. These three brilliant actors will bring to life a moment like the one captured in that photograph.

The dialogue between the actors playing Malcolm and Martin is nothing short of outstanding. These two famous men are often contrasted and compared. Both are imagined as meeting at the height of their public careers — both destined to die for a cause larger than themselves.

Said the Rev. King, "Procrastination is still the thief of time. Over the bleached bones and jumbled residues of numerous civilizations are written the pathetic words 'too late.'"

This evening, we hope that this play will inspire the audience to act before it's too late.

A Luta Continua, which means in Portuguese that the struggle continues.

Carl Snowden: History must be understood, not buried

January 23, 2018

Leonard Blackshear and I shared an appreciation of history — a belief it was not only important but interrelated and intertwined.

We were approached in 1999 by William F. Chaney, who wanted to build a statue in Lothian in honor of one of his ancestors, Pvt. Benjamin Welch Owens, who fought for the Confederacy. Bill Chaney was passionate about his Southern heritage, did not hold President Abraham Lincoln in high esteem and referred to the Civil War as an "invasion" by Northerners. He truly believed the wrong side lost the war.

Lewis Bracy, a Hanover community activist, said at the time, "Any tribute to the Confederacy would be celebrating evil — no different than a tribute to the German army."

Mr Chaney's response: "This boy wasn't fighting for slavery. He was fighting for states' rights and his country." You couldn't have had more of a racial divide.

I became friends with "Billy," as I called him. We would spend hours on the telephone or over dinner talking about race and politics.

He joined the NAACP, becoming a life member, and convinced Mr. Blackshear, who died in 2006, to attend and speak at the ceremony that unveiled the statute. That statue stands to this day at a church in Lothian.

Billy used his own money to build that statue, remains proud of his Southern heritage — yet also supported our efforts to build the Alex Haley-Kunta Kinte Memorial and put up a plaque honoring Malcolm X in Annapolis.

Recently, I became aware that the Cavaliers home — one of the largest homes in Lothian when it was built by Philip Thomas in 1804 — is on the market. According to Mr. Chaney, it has a rich history that will be lost unless the state or the county purchases it.

I share his concern about the loss of history, which needs to be preserved and placed in context, not whitewashed or sanitized.

Next week brings the start of Black History Month. As I and others have argued, "black history" is American history. They are interrelated and connected. Many are unaware that Thomas Jefferson had black descendants just as Malcolm X had white relatives. American history is a melting pot in more ways than one.

Some believe it's better to forget the past and look to the future. I respectfully disagree. We shouldn't forget Hitler and the Holocaust. Dee Brown's book about the treatment of Native Americans, "Bury My Heart at Wounded Knee," should be required reading in Anne Arundel County Public Schools. Historic structures — whether the Cavaliers home in Lothian or the Eastport Colored School in Annapolis — should be preserved.

Our children need to know all of their history — a history in which race and racism continue to be sensitive subjects.

At the time of the controversy over the statue of Pvt. Benjamin Welch Owens, then-County Executive Janet S. Owens said, "You can't deny your history... the more we talk about it and explore the good and the bad, the healthier it is for everyone."

History is nothing more than a diary recording some of our most personal thoughts. Yet, if we are ever going to be honest with one another, that starts not with burying our history but with understanding it. If we do so, young people will understand why nooses, swastikas, lynchings, gas chambers, concentration camps, internment camps and forced segregation all are a part of our history.

They will better understand what then-U.S. Senator Barack Obama meant in 2008 when he gave his famous "A More Perfect Union" speech in Philadelphia. They will understand why President Ronald Reagan received such applause for saying "Tear down this wall" — and another president who said "build the wall" has come under such great criticism.

It will also help readers to understand the words, *A Luta Continua*, which in Portuguese means that the struggle continues.

Carl Snowden: Fundraiser for Capital Gazette memorial set for Wednesday

September 24, 2018

On June 28, a delegation of the Caucus of African-American Leaders were meeting with Mayor Gavin Buckley when we learned of the shocking news that five people were slain in the Capital-Gazette newsroom. Although it has been almost three months since that horrific and life-changing moment, many of us continue to grieve.

Those of us gathered around the mayor's conference table had worked with Wendi Winters, Rob Hiaasen, John McNamara, Rebecca Smith, and Gerald Fischman. Gerald edited my columns and I saw Wendi on a regular basis. We went to the same gym.

Our dilemma was how to honor the memory of the journalists and not the heinous act? Shortly after their deaths, Juanita Cage Lewis who knew Wendi Winters contacted me and recommended that the Caucus of African-American Leaders and the Dr. Martin Luther King, Jr. Committee do something so that these people would not have died in vain.

I contacted Daryl Jones, a former member of the Anne Arundel County Council and a lawyer and we decided that creating a memorial in their memory would be a fitting and lasting tribute. We decided that the mantra "A Free Society begins with a free press" would be our capital fundraising campaign slogan.

We got the unanimous approval of the board of directors of the non-profit Dr. Martin Luther King Jr. Committee, which I chair to become a partner and the Baltimore Media Group which owns The Capital to allow us to go forward with this project.

The Dr. Martin Luther King, Jr. Committee has successfully led three capital fundraising campaign projects that created the Dr. Martin Luther King, Jr. Memorial at Anne Arundel Community College, the Coretta Scott King Memorial Garden in Edgewater and the Civil Rights Foot Soldiers Memorial in Annapolis.

Each of these memorials were funded by private donors and donated to Anne Arundel Community College and the City of Annapolis. The groups involved decided to build a Capital Gazette Freedom of the Press Memorial dedicated to the principle of the First Amendment and the journalists who were murdered while performing their jobs.

Mayor Buckley appointed members of his staff to find a suitable site for this memorial in our city. A select subcommittee of the Dr. Martin Luther King Jr. Committee has been charged with spearheading this effort.

Members of that subcommittee include Alderwoman Elly Tierney, Attorney Daryl Jones, Dee Goodwyn, Juanita Cage Lewis, Judge Vickie Gipson, Mary Grace Gallagher, and Marion Wenn.

Joining us will be Alan J. Hyatt, Dana Vickers Shelley, executive director of the ACLU of Maryland, Alderwoman Rhonda Pindell Charles, John Brassel, Bob Mosier, Jennifer Alexander, Scott McMullen, Alice Johnson Cain, Stacie Wollman, Dimitri Sfakiyanudis, Jeff Henderson, Emile Henault, Argo Duenas, Shane Nikolao, Melanie Smith, journalists, and a cadre of supporters of the First Amendment, who believes that a free press is essential to a democracy.

Wednesday, we will pause to pay tribute to The Capital employees who lost their lives. The proposed Capital Gazette Freedom of the Press Memorial will be a permanent reminder that a person may murder journalists but they will never kill journalism, because, the right to speak, to publish, to broadcast, to protest, will exist as long as there is an America.

The journalists who died on June 28, like the founders of this nation, knew that presidents come and go, however, the First Amendment is sacred and in honoring these journalists we honor the best that our nation has to offer.

A Luta Continua, which in Portuguese means that the struggle continues for freedom of the press, justice, and peace, must never cease. A free society begins with a free press.

Carl Snowden: What a year 2018 has been for change in Anne Arundel

December 10, 2018

What a year 2018 has been! As we prepare for the upcoming New Year, there have been so many things that have occurred in this year.

This month marks the anniversary of Mayor Gavin Buckley's first year in office.

Like newly elected County Executive Steuart Pittman, Mayor Buckley had never held public office. Both Buckley and Pittman are neophytes who have been given a mandate.

Voters clearly wanted the city and county to move in a different direction. Having served in public office, I am quite aware of the difference between politicking and governing.

Voters give their elected officials a honeymoon, but, it doesn't last long. I am a great admirer of people who seek to serve the public. Public service can be both a blessing and a curse. I have had the privilege of serving in government at the city, county and state level. I know what good governance can produce.

I am fully aware that there would be no Alex Haley-Kunta Kinte Memorial in downtown Annapolis, a Civil Rights Foot Soldiers Memorial at Whitmore Park or the only Dr. Martin Luther King, Jr, Memorial in the State of Maryland, had we not elected to public office men and women who understood that government that is inclusive will have capital projects that serve all segments of the community.

When I met with candidate Steuart Pittman, I made it clear that I was not seeking a job in his administration. What I was seeking from him is what the vast majority of voters and taxpayers want a government that is efficient and responsive.

I believe that the reason voters voted for change in the last two elections is that they wanted people that understand that they are public servants and not wedded to private enterprises.

Voters want people who understand that they work for them and not the other way around. During the midterm elections, I believe we have elected a number of progressive officials who believe in the principle that government works best when there is a seat at the table for everyone,

I believe our recently elected local government officials will be more civil and respectful to the people it serves. Racism, sexism, antisemitism and other forms of bigotry will not be tolerated.

This became clear when Councilwoman Lisa Rodvien, state Senator-elect Sarah Elfreth and Delegate-elect Alice Cain joined the Caucus of African-American Leaders, Action Annapolis, Anne Arundel Indivisible, Showing up for Racial Justice Anne Arundel, Annapolis, Connecting the Dots, NAACP and WISE came together to condemn the unacceptable Facebook postings of a newly appointed Board of Education member.

I believe that the newly elected members of the County Council along with County Executive Pittman will set a tone of civility that will make all of us proud.

Carl Snowden: Remembering Elijah Cummings

October 10, 2019

Tick. Tock. Tick. Tock. It is Saturday and it's time to get on the school bus. The bell has rung and school is now in session.

This week's lesson is about an anti-Ku Klux Klan march in Annapolis, Maryland that the late Congressman Elijah Cummings participated in 1998.

Over two decades ago, the Ku Klux Klan had announced that they were marching in Annapolis. I was involved in organizing the counter-demonstration.

We decided that it was important to have political leaders participate in the anti-Klan march to demonstrate to the Klan that they didn't have a scintilla of support. We recruited Maryland Governor Parris N. Glendenning, U.S. Senator Barbara A. Mikulski, and Congressman Cummings.

They were on the frontline as we joined arms in solidarity against the White supremacists in February of that year. I had known Congressman Cummings when he was a delegate serving in the Maryland General Assembly. I met him via the late Congressman Parren J. Mitchell, who had introduced us years earlier. We had remained allies ever since.

Over the years my admiration for Congressman Cummings grew. He had spoken in Annapolis on numerous occasions. He keynoted both the annual Dr. Martin Luther King, Jr. Awards Dinner and Dr. Martin Luther King, Jr. Memorial Breakfast. At each of these events, he never failed to remind audiences of the damage that racism did to his people.

He used to tell his audience how he was placed in "Special Education." How people thought that he was "slow". How people assumed that his pigmentation was a liability. It was not. He was a great storyteller. He once said that his purpose on earth was to lift people up. Congressman Cummings said, "I don't want to die without doing everything that I can to lift people up."

Donnell Harris and Cyrus Scott sent me a video recording where Congressman Cummings makes that point over and over again.

In it, he says what would a preacher be without a congregation? What would a teacher be without a student?

By this time next week, Congressman Cummings will be buried. A week from today, the media will have done their final stories. Already the discussion is "who will replace him" in Congress? He like his predecessor Congressman Parren J. Mitchell will not be "replaced," rather someone will succeed them.

Men and women like them are never "replaced." They come to us like a rising star. My memories of him are many. Marching, speaking, crying, demanding, cajoling and in the latter part of his life in a wheelchair and on a walker.

His predecessor Congressman Mitchell ironically was in the same situation.

I remember that great line that Reverend Jesse Jackson once said about another wheelchair-bound leader: "I would rather have Roosevelt in a wheelchair than Reagan on a horse," he said. My sentiments were the same about Elijah.

Few could imagine more than two decades ago the man that marched in that consequential march in Annapolis would be in a wheelchair and requiring the use of a walker to move about.

Yet, in Washington, D.C. he would continue speaking against illicit policies that were being promulgated by the man in the White House.

When someone dies, there is a tendency through a eulogy, to sum up, a person's life. In truth, no matter, how great the eulogist, no one every captures an individual in their entirety.

Yet, like a photograph, you can capture a moment. He marched for a cause greater than himself, standing with the power brokers of his day."

Life and death will intersect in everyone's journey. There will come a time when the clock will stop for us all. There will come a time when the tick-tock of life stops.

Last April, he spoke so eloquently for the last time at the West County Democratic Club's Annual Parren J. Mitchell dinner in Anne Arundel County, Maryland.

I saw him on that walker approaching the podium after being introduced by a prominent attorney and former Councilman Daryl Jones.

As he spoke to an audience that included Anne Arundel County Executive Steuart Pittman, Delegate Shaneka Henson, Delegate Alice Cain, Delegate Mike Rogers, Delegate Sandy Bartlett, Councilman Andrew Pruski, and other newly elected officials and bellowed that "we are better than that."

The "better than that" was in referenced to the policies of President Donald Trump that separated families, divided Americans and polarized the nation.

They rose to their feet to applaud the man and his message. I looked around the room that night. I saw the men and women that he inspired Juanita Cage Lewis, Larry Diggs, Andrea Horton, Gloria Criss, Jacqueline Allsup, Dee Goodwyn, Christine Davenport, Antonio Downing, Reverend Dr. Diane Dixon-Proctor, Charles E James Sr., Patrick Armstrong, Cynthia Abney Carter, Tryphenia A. Ellis-Johnson, Ruby Singleton Blakeney, Thea Boykins-Wilson, Eugene Peterson, Thornell Jones, J.t. Sharps, Tony J. Spencer, Jeff Henderson, Kenneth Kirby, Sylvia Barnett, Sylvia Harris and Janice Hayes-Williams to name just a few.

I thought about the pain that he was enduring. The difficulties that he was experiencing. The trouble that he had walking. Six months later, it all came to an end.

God in his infinite wisdom called Elijah home. No more marches, no more insults, no more battles, no more sleepless nights. God decided that it was time for Elijah to join a special place that freedom fighters and warriors go.

In this place, he will meet Parren Mitchell, Thurgood Marshall, Harriett Tubman, Frederick Douglass - all Marylanders. Also, he will see Malcolm, Martin, Maya, and Mandela.

He will find himself assembled with those who came before him.

Every march has a goal. Every moment is an opportunity to help somebody.

In the end, it is indeed not your status, bank account or title that determines whether you sit with the Angels, it is your service.

This history lesson isn't just about a man, it is about a movement. It is not about being first or being last, it is about service.

I remember my mentor and friend, the late Reverend Dr. Leroy Bowman telling me that when his day comes, what he would like to have people say about him. He said, "I don't want people to look down in my casket and say 'Reverend Bowman sure looks good', I want them to say, 'he was a good man."

When Congressman Elijah Cummings died, we lost a "good man." His funeral will be on Friday, his legacy and place in history is already secured.

He has fought the good battle, marched for the last time. He will be remembered by some and forgotten by others.

For me, what will always be important is that I saw him smile. I saw him stand tall. I saw him inspire a new generation of leaders. I know that he made life better for many.

He taught us all how in the face of great difficulties, to keep marching. Never let them break your spirit.

The class bell is ringing class is over. See you next Saturday and remember, "We are better than that".

A Luta Continua!

EPILOGUE

I hope that this book will become the catalyst for my own autobiography. It has taken longer than I initially thought. In many ways, it has allowed me to have a greater appreciation for what goes into writing a book. It is my hope that the reader will be inspired by the stories contained within.

In many ways, this book is dedicated to the men and women who will never see or read it. I am fortunate to have had the opportunity to write this book and share my views on a whole host of issues.

I believe that every human being has a story to tell. Far too many will never do so and because of that fact, our world is lacking those voices, which is precisely why this book is dedicated to them.

I leave you with the words "A Luta Continua" which in Portuguese means that the struggle continues.

Printed in the United States
By Bookmasters